A LIFELONG FRIEND

Discovering God's Faithfulness
When You Feel Broken

LAUREL KASCO

HIGHERLIFE
PUBLISHING & MARKETING

Cover photo and styling by Leigh Thompson.

Higher Life Publishing & Marketing
P.O. Box 623307 Oviedo, FL 32762
www.higherlifepublishing.com

Ordering Information: Quantity sales. Special discounts are available on quantity purchases by corporations, associations, and others. For details, contact the publisher.

ISBN Paperback - 9798989529421
ISBN ebook - 9798989529438
LOC: 1-13563884849

Printed in the United States of America.

Contents

Acknowledgements

I want to thank my parents, Bob and Gloria Costa, for being a constant help and support on this long journey of life. I thank all my friends and family, including: Sean and Emma Kasco for encouraging and strengthening me to finish this project strong; Candice Costa, Leigh Thompson, and Zach Bush, M.D., for the sound advice and support you always bring; and Juan Ochoa, M.D., for researching and caring. I'm so grateful for the entire team at A HigherLife Publishing, Esse, my editor, and Virginia, my book manager. Thank you, Brian Faircloth, Tanya Brown, and Julie Futrell for your prayers and especially your friendship; and Pastor Carlos Sarmiento for sharing your biblical knowledge and expertise as I attempted to write about an infinite God. Finally, my heartfelt thanks to everyone who volunteered for the book launch or review team, and everyone who prayed for or encouraged me during this process over the last eighteen years.

Dedication

First, I dedicate this book to God, my faithful Friend who inspired me to write it; for every broken heart who needs to know God loves you and wants to help—no matter what; and to my grandmother and grandfather, Patricia Costa and Robert Costa Sr., for all their support, and for encouraging me to write my story to benefit others.

Introduction

Dear Reader,

As you read this book, I hope and pray you come to know how much God cares about every detail of your life. He truly wants to hang out with you and be your best Friend.

Life is often like a roller coaster. Sometimes things are great, and sometimes trauma and hardship catch you by surprise.

In my early twenties, I went through a dark, challenging season. There were times God seemed distant and that I couldn't hear Him. Instead, I heard Satan loud and clear. For a time, he convinced me that I had gone too far, and all hope was lost because I had screwed up my life too much for God to help me. Then, one day, I cried out to God, and everything changed!

I hope as you read about the journey I have had with God, you will discover how He wants to be your Friend, too! He wants to extend His love to you in all the moments throughout your life, but He often waits for you to ask Him for help and Friendship. God is always ready to run to help you, so the moment you invite Him to be the Friend and Lord of your life, He will. Then He will wrap you in a warm blanket of His love. He already knows everything about you, and He still loves you more than you can imagine!

God is good, faithful, kind, loving, just, honorable, and is not shaken by the storms we often face. Nothing is too hard for Him; God is all-powerful and wants to encourage you to never give up! No matter what your life looks like, remember, God wants to be the Friend who sticks closer than a brother.

Proverbs 18:24

Sincerely,

Laurel Kasco

Chapter 1

God My Friend

> *The man of too many friends [chosen*
> *indiscriminately] will be broken in pieces*
> *and come to ruin, but there is a [true, loving]*
> *friend who [is reliable and] sticks closer than*
> *a brother.* (Proverbs 18:24)

She bullied other kids, too, but this one teacher really seemed to have it in for me. Every day she found reason to punish me with humiliation, shouting without warning, stuffing soap in my mouth till I almost choked, and even striking my hands with a wooden paddle as I cried and cried. I was four years old. I should have said something to my mother or father but, for some reason, I didn't.

In a way, I'm glad. How else would I have known that God is real? To this day, Mom doesn't know exactly what prompted her to grab me in the middle of the school day never to return, but I knew. God had heard my cry, begging Him to save me from the bully teacher and the school that seemed to always turn a blind eye. Since that very day, I knew that God is real, and I knew without a doubt that He sees, He hears, and He is my Friend.

As of this writing, I am forty-one, and if I were to fill this entire book with accounts of the miracles, encounters, and times I've had with God, I would barely scratch the surface. If you can relate to that, then you understand. **If you can't relate, then I'm really glad you're here.** Stay with me to the end, and your life will never be the same.

Romans 2:11 promises us, "God does not show favoritism." The Father, Son, and Holy Spirit will not take better care of me than you. They will not show me mercy and kindness, or grant me deliverance, healing, or blessings that They will not also grant you. What God has done for me, He'll do for you. I pray that as you read my story, you encounter the Father. See God with you in your circumstances like He was in mine. If you love how God showed up for me, ask Him to do it for you. Ask and you shall receive! Pay attention to the details and you will find that He is everywhere all the time dropping little (and large) signposts of His love for you. If you're just being yourself, you can't possibly miss it. God made you. He speaks your language and He knows how to meet you more than halfway. Only ask, and be alert for His answer.

Come Away...

> *My beloved speaks and says to me, "Arise, my love, my fair one, and come away."*
> (Song of Solomon 2:10)

Regular, debilitating seizures had me questioning whether I could ever hope to enjoy my life. Could it be I somehow failed to qualify for the "abundant life" Jesus promised in Scripture? I was years into these seizures, but nothing manmade was able stop the attacks on my brain and body. I knew God would have to intervene on my behalf for me to be well again.

At this time in my life, I was no longer completely destitute. I had fellowship. I was going to church. I was praying regularly and eating healthy and actively seeking God.

Then Jesus said, "Let's go off by ourselves to a
quiet place and rest awhile."
(Mark 6:31 NLT)

I said yes. Jesus had heard my heart's cry and responded by providing a way for me to be alone with Him for a month-long sabbatical.

As you walk with God, sometimes He gives you an inkling that He's up to something—like a bride being prepared for that one special moment that changes everything. A single encounter with God can transform you and your whole life forever. During this time alone together—just me and God—I felt every day bringing us deeper in intimacy, and every passing hour pull some unimaginable, momentous encounter with God towards me.

On March 7, 2004, I was grateful to have someone who could take me to church. I couldn't drive due to the epilepsy, which meant I could rarely attend. Just being able to go at all made the day special.

I will always remember that morning's message. A pastor named Jacobs preached on Moses's journey and the trials that preceded his life-altering encounter with God at the burning bush. I took in every word like it was bread for my soul, coming to life within me.

"You went through painful trials and even sickness, and God has taught you in the midst of your sufferings…"

It was as if Jacobs spoke to me directly.

I knew that God didn't *cause* the sickness in my body. I knew He didn't "will" the abuse or emotional pain, because God is our Healer and Deliverer. He provides a way even when all the plans of man fail. I may have suffered, but I learned and grew stronger in the fiery trials, and I sensed that my time to come out of the fire was just around the corner.

"…but He is going to deliver you!"

I believed it just as I heard it. As Jacobs preached, my spirit witnessed the word was coming through the mouth of a man but from the heart of God, so I agreed in trust that God would see me through to complete healing of my body and deliverance for my life.

Just Say Yes

When you trust a loving Father, you don't always have to understand what He is asking of you or calling you to do. I had begun a practice of simply saying yes to God on a regular basis; so, when Pastor Jacobs gave an altar call, I said yes again. I had been weeping during the message be-cause it was so real to me. Hungry for more of God, I made my way toward the altar. I had no special request. I simply raised my arms in surrender and said, "Yes, Lord, yes."

I stood in the line spanning the front of the sanctuary as the pastor made his way through, praying for people one by one, but I wasn't waiting for him. I focused only on God and being in His presence. It was of no concern to me whether I received prayer because I knew that God Himself could touch me right where I stood—and He did.

Suddenly, I sensed that Jesus was standing directly in front of me. I don't mean that I simply felt God's presence in a powerful way. I mean that I knew Jesus the Son of God was standing right in front of me, in person. I couldn't see Him, but I knew He was there. Waterworks unleashed as I wept. My body crumpled like a leaf to the floor. (It sounds crazy. My husband used to think it was crazy until this happened to *him* one night!)

I wasn't worried about falling, crying, or what anyone else thought of me. At that moment, I was meeting with the Father, Son, and Holy Spirit, and nothing else mattered.

As I laid on the carpet in the front of the sanctuary, God's power and presence rested on me so heavily that I was unable to move; yet, my whole heart and mind maintained perfect focus on Him.

Clearly, I heard the Father say, "I was walking in your midst, and Jesus came to you and touched you."

That's exactly how it felt.

As He continued, He opened my eyes to see into the spiritual realm, showing me a video of what I had just experienced. I saw God from behind, walking through the crowd. I could see His outline while the rest of His body looked almost clear or invisible.

This alone would have been enough for me, but it was not the end of the encounter. As I laid there, I could sense a battle taking place. It reminded me of Jacob when he wrestled with God.

*So Jacob was left alone, and a man wrestled
with him till daybreak.... Then the man said,
"Let me go, for it is daybreak." But Jacob
replied, "I will not let you go unless you bless
me."*

*Then the man said, "...you have struggled
with God and with humans and have
overcome."* (Genesis 32:24, 25, 27–28 NIV)

So, I said in my heart: *I am not leaving until I get my miracle!*

Well, I couldn't move anyway because God's power was still
resting on me. As I continued to wait in stillness, He began
to show me pictures of how He saw me and of things He
planned for me in the future. I saw myself with beautiful
long hair that glistened in the light as if millions of tiny
diamonds were woven through it. He turned the picture
around so I could see my face. It looked like me, but made
of pure gold. Going through the fire purifies us like gold.
The picture was symbolic of the work God had done in my
life, and of my value to Him.

That was not at all how I had seen myself. For years I struggled with feeling worthless. God wanted me to know how
I looked through His eyes. He saw great potential when
everyone else saw a mess.

I felt His hand on my body, moving from one area to another. Wherever He touched became extremely hot. As I
stayed unmoving, lying in His presence, completely forgetful of the building and the scenery around me, He caught
me up even higher with Him and showed me a movie of

my life in days to come. This was so real that it was like I was watching it all happen live. In total, I was caught up with God for about three and a half hours.

Normally, the other church attendees would have left much earlier, but as God would have it, this was the first Sunday of the month, and on the first Sunday, the congregation always enjoyed a fellowship lunch after second service. Their lingering fellowship afforded me more uninterrupted time for my encounter. He always makes a way.

Knowing it was God that held me there, and probably not daring to interfere, Pastor asked some women to stay behind to watch over me. Even after the three and a half hours, I was still so caught up with God that I had to have assistance standing up and gradually moving again.

Later, Pastor Jacobs explained that God had shown Him what was happening to me—that I'd been in a battle against a spirit of infirmity and won. He saw that I had come out of the fire "as pure gold." It was a perfect affirmation of what God showed me in the vision. Pastor also saw by the Spirit that I had wrestled with God like Jacob. Isn't it funny that his name was *Jacobs*?

We both had confirmation and assurance of just how real that life-altering encounter was.

Just like in Jacob's Bible story, I would not let go of God that day until I had my miracle and, just like Jacob, He gave it to me.

Be encouraged as you read this because God cares about you. On the cross, He showed you He would go to any length and endure any pain just to have you in His love and care. He will take the time to meet with you on this level as you continue to seek Him with even a little faith, never giving up. I didn't get a microwave miracle. I listened to God's voice over time. I said yes to Him instead of trying to do everything my way. This is why Christ becomes our rest. Without Him, we try and try and try and fail. As you'll see in the pages ahead, the best thing you can do is what Jesus says in this passage:

> *Come to Me, all who are weary and heavily burdened [by religious rituals that provide no peace], and I will give you rest [refreshing your souls with salvation].*

> *Take My yoke upon you and learn from Me [following Me as My disciple], for I am gentle and humble in heart, and you will find rest (renewal, blessed quiet) FOR YOUR SOULS.*

> *For My yoke is easy [to bear] and My burden is light.* (Matthew 11:28–30)

Chapter 2

In His Presence

...believe that God exists and that He
rewards those who [earnestly and diligently]
seek Him. (Hebrews 11:6b)

Encounters like the one I shared aren't easy to explain and may be hard to believe, but seek Him anyway with all your heart and all your strength, and you will be rewarded. Just one meeting, one encounter, one touch from the Living God, can change everything—forever.

The day I laid on that church floor for over three hours was the very day I started moving on with my life. I didn't have to be super religious or get my behavior just right. I simply had been longing to meet with God. He heard my prayers and showed up in such a powerful way that it changed the very course of my life.

God wants to meet with you.

If you'll let Him, God will do whatever it takes to restore you. After many months and years of suffering, I got up off that floor filled with the hope and encouragement I desperately needed to continue towards my destiny.

Even though this is the biggest meeting with God I had ever experienced, it was not the first, nor would it be the last. In 2001, years before my encounter at the altar surrounded by people, I'd had one in my room on my bed all by myself ... well, sort of alone.

The Train of His Robe

> *I saw [in a vision] the Lord sitting on a throne, high and exalted, with the train of His royal robe filling the [most holy part of the] temple.* (Isaiah 6:1)

Every passing hour carried a heavier blow of pounding, excruciating pain. I took some Tylenol, but it didn't faze this migraine. When the throbbing seemed too much to bear, I retired in bed with a towel on my chest and a trash can nearby in case I had to throw up. For hours I prayed for God to forgive every time I missed, ignored, or disobeyed His instructions.

I remembered the woman who was healed in Mark 5:24–34:

> *…She had spent all that she had and was not helped at all, but instead had become worse.*
>
> *She had heard [reports] about Jesus, and she came up behind Him in the crowd and touched His outer robe. For she thought, "If I just touch His clothing, I will get well."*
>
> *Immediately her flow of blood was dried up; and she felt in her body [and knew without any doubt] that she was healed….*
>
> *Then He said to her, "Daughter, your faith [your personal trust and confidence in Me] has restored you to health; go in peace and be*

[permanently] healed from your suffering.
(Mark 5:26–29, 34)

At about the four-hour mark of asking God if I could just touch the hem of Jesus's robe, I suddenly felt God's presence sweep through my room with a gust of wind. In with the presence came the train of a large robe that filled my room tangibly from left to right. I felt it cover me like a blanket. The "presence" was Jesus.

I saw Satan's dark eyes, and then, just like that—he was gone. My migraine vanished, too, as the Spirit showed me that all the pain and torment I'd been enduring were satanic attacks.

Thicker and stronger His presence grew in my room until I felt like I was in heaven and on earth at the same time. All my pain was gone. I continued to worship with singing, but it was more than that. It seemed I worshiped not just with my voice or from my emotions, but as if my whole being reached towards God in love and adoration. I sensed that worship in heaven was something like this.

I had two visions of my future, and inherently I knew that I could only fulfill those visions by staying close with God and putting Him first in every aspect of my life.

After the visions, I picked up a pen and began to write as God downloaded words of revelations and prophecies. The experience of God opening you to hear truth and promises and future events is nothing short of exhilarating! It hardly even matters what God is saying so long as He is the one speaking. Later, I shared it with my parents and the rabbi from our Messianic Jewish synagogue and we celebrated God's miracles together.

I am not better than anyone else or more important in God's eyes. I just go after God and will not let go until I get my blessing. I pray like the woman in Jesus's parable in Luke:

> *Now Jesus was telling the disciples a parable*
> *to make the point that at all times they ought*
> *to pray and not give up and lose heart, saying,*
>
> *"In a certain city there was a judge who*
> *did not fear God and had no respect for*
> *man. There was a [desperate] widow in that*
> *city and she kept coming to him and saying,*
> *'Give me justice and legal protection from my*
> *adversary.'*
>
> *"For a time he would not; but later he*
> *said to himself, 'Even though I do not*
> *fear God nor respect man, yet because this*
> *widow continues to bother me, I will give*
> *her justice and legal protection; otherwise by*
> *continually coming she [will be an intolerable*
> *annoyance and she] will wear me out.'"*
>
> *Then the Lord said, "Listen to what the*
> *unjust judge says! And will not [our just] God*
> *defend and avenge His elect [His chosen*
> *ones] who cry out to Him day and night?*

*"Will He delay [in providing justice] on their
behalf?*

*"I tell you that He will defend and avenge
them quickly. However, when the Son
of Man comes, will He find [this kind of
persistent] faith on the earth?"*
(Luke 18:1–8)

The unjust judge didn't care what happened to the widow
but grew so sick of hearing her petition that he granted her
justice only to get rid of her. Jesus says God will "defend
and avenge" us quickly, but warns that He may not find us
watching for His answer "persistently" in faith. God may
come, but if we stop believing, if we turn our backs on God,
we won't see His hand reaching to pull us out of the ditch.

God does care, and He will not ignore us when we come
to Him asking, seeking, and knocking on the door of His
heart for help. Even through a difficult process, as we continue to believe, God restores us, makes us stronger, and
takes us closer to the final manifestation of healing.

*And not only this, but [with joy] let us exult
in our sufferings and rejoice in our hardships,
knowing that hardship (distress, pressure,
trouble) produces patient endurance; and
endurance, proven character (spiritual
maturity);*

*and proven character, hope and confident
assurance [of eternal salvation].*

> *Such hope [in God's promises] never*
> *disappoints us, because God's love has been*
> *abundantly poured out within our hearts*
> *through the Holy Spirit who was given to us.*
>   (Romans 5:3–5)

The Invitation

Do you only hang out with your friends when you are in trouble or in need?

No.

You invite them over for dinner. You laugh, hang out, go to the movies, the beach, and concerts. You do life together because you enjoy being with them. You pick up the phone to call your friends, so why not take a moment today to talk to your Lifelong Friend?

You don't need to be "super spiritual" or spend hours in silence praying and fasting to know His love. God is real and personal. He wants to have an intimate relationship with you. He's not just here to show up in the nick of time during a crisis. Every day He wants to reveal Himself to you in new ways.

I encourage you today: ask Jesus to be the Lord and leader of your life. Ask God to fill you with the Holy Spirit and to send you friends who know Him as well. Decide you will go after God until you hear from Him directly. Right now, you can experience His wonderful presence and friendship for yourself. Only ask!

Chapter 3

Rescued

> *He sent from above, He took me; He drew me*
> *out of great waters. He rescued me from my*
> *strong enemy, from those who had hated me,*
> *for they were too mighty for me.*
> (2 Samuel 22:17–18)

I like this verse because it depicts being in deep waters, a metaphor for being in trouble so deep you could never save yourself. While our spiritual battles often *manifest* through people, people are not our real enemies. Our enemy is Satan and his demons.

> *For our struggle is not against flesh and*
> *blood [contending only with physical*
> *opponents], but against the rulers, against*
> *the powers, against the world forces*
> *of this [present] darkness, against the*
> *spiritual forces of wickedness in the heavenly*
> *(supernatural) places.* (Ephesians 6:12)

The ocean isn't my enemy. The ocean is full of energy and force. It can overwhelm me. The waves and currents are often too mighty for me. Sometimes our struggle comes through people or direct spiritual attack. Other times, it is just the forces of nature.

I'm astounded by how many times God has protected and held me up by the power of His right hand. Rescues like these could happen to anyone on any day. As you read about these miracles, may God reveal to you His constant involvement in your daily life.

Ocean Rescue

I was born in Florida. When I was nine, our family moved to a little village in the Ohio River Valley known as Higginsport, and sometimes Dad brought us back to Florida to visit relatives and enjoy vacations.

Of course, we always went to the beach. Even if it wasn't summertime, it still felt warm to us compared to Ohio's freezing cold winter.

During one trip, I put on my swimsuit and headed down to the ocean. A lifeguard was nearby so I felt safe wading into the water a couple feet deep. It was windy and overcast and I knew not to go out far. The salty breeze whipped my long blonde hair in all directions. I turned my face into the wind so it would blow my hair back. Slowly and carefully, I stepped further into the water till I was immersed up to my knees. This seemed perfectly safe.

Suddenly, there was no ground.

The water temperature dropped substantially, and the currents gripped me. I found myself sucked down into frigid water deeper and deeper. In the span of two seconds, I was plunged probably seven feet under. Instinctively, I reached my arm up as high as I could stretch it, hoping someone would see and pull me out.

No one saw.

In a flash, I had vanished.

My last clear thought was, *Help, pull me out!* but I couldn't scream. I would never be heard. I was completely alone as the cold dark water swallowed me whole.

Everything went black.

Time seemed to slow down while death had me in its grasp, but barely an instant had passed before my outstretched hand was met by a firm grip.

I awoke on the beach lying peacefully in shallow water. An ocean that moments prior was violent and dangerous was now gently washing over my skin. My breathing was normal. I was not hurt. After a few deep inhales, I realized that someone had come to my rescue, and that whoever it was had not only taken me from the deep waters but also placed me safely on the sand.

Who pulled me out?!

I sat up straight and looked around. No one was in view except a lifeguard perched high on his red lifeguard seat, still laughing and talking to a friend as if nothing had happened.

It was all so fast. I was sucked down until the water was way over my head, then pulled out, and then placed on the beach all within less than one minute. As I lay there in shock, cold and soaking wet, I realized that God had sent an angel to pull me out of the water.

> *For He will command His angels in regard to*
> *you, to protect and defend and guard you in*
> *all your ways [of obedience and service]. They*
> *will lift you up in their hands, so that you do*
> *not [even] strike your foot against a stone.*
> (Psalm 91:11–12)

Wow! I wished I hadn't blacked out for the rescue. I would have loved to see the angel. Mostly, I was amazed at God's nearness. I was dragged into darkness till I was in over my head with no one to save me, but God, my best Friend, heard my cry and sent an angel to rescue me.

Later that day I went back down to the beach, but this time with my younger sister.

"Be careful," I warned her, though she hadn't the slightest idea why I was being so protective.

"Come here," she urged, impatient with my cautious protests. "I want to show you something."

"This is dangerous," I replied. "I almost drowned here this morning." I proceeded to explain how I had come upon a sudden drop-off that sucked me in and pulled me down with a current too strong for me to resist.

Thinking me dramatic, she laughed.

I followed her to a specific spot she wanted to show me. It was the drop-off! Once again, there was no more ocean floor for my feet to grab, and once again I was going down fast; but this time, the aggressive whirlpool was gone and I was able to overcome it.

My sister laughed even harder now. I can see why. It seemed funny that time, but it was near-death earlier.

In moments when no one is around to help, we cry out anyway and God Himself shows up to rescue and protect us. Angels are real. They serve God, perhaps like demons serve Satan.

Has God ever personally and supernaturally rescued you from a dangerous situation?

221

There is a road near Higginsport, Ohio, called the 221. The 221 is no joke. It's a windy, curvy, uphill road, uneven and full of twists, turns, and drop-offs as you work your way up towards Georgetown. I had traveled this road during all seasons of Ohio weather and knew it well.

One winter day, I was heading up 221 to Georgetown, most likely for a house cleaning or babysitting job. As I reached the summit of a small hill and began descending, I found that suddenly all four of my tires were on solid black ice. I completely lost control. My car swung to the right, zig-zagged left, jerked to the right again sharply, and had me heading straight for the steep cliff into a creek. There was nothing I could do but watch.

At the very moment I realized I had no control, an invisible hand grabbed my steering wheel. Immediately, the tires straightened, the jerking stopped, and my car swung perfectly inside my driving lane as if nothing had happened.

Whew! It was a close call but God rescued me again, even with no time to think or pray as I slid all over that solid black ice.

> *And we know [with great confidence] that*
> *God [who is deeply concerned about us] causes*
> *all things to work together [as a plan] for good*
> *for those who love God, to those who are called*
> *according to His plan and purpose.*
>   (Romans 8:28)

What could have been a major and disastrous car accident turned into another miracle. Relieved, I completed my drive up the big hill into Georgetown safely.

The 221 was dangerous to drive, but I had to brave it to reach my destination. Likewise, sometimes life takes you down a dangerous road and there's just no other way towards your destiny. If you do hit solid ice, literally or figuratively, you'll need Jesus to take the wheel, too! Don't wait until tragedy nearly strikes before you strike up a relationship with God. Walk in regular, daily relationship, and you will find these and more unexpected blessings fill your life.

German Shepherd Rescue

Not long after we moved to Ohio, our family got a puppy and we named him Spotty. He was an English Setter bird dog. My younger sister trained him through 4-H, and he listened very well. He was a huge part of our family and our daily life for many years.

Years later, I was already a young adult. Spotty wasn't as energetic but still seemed to like being with us. He was getting older and had an eye injury from running into a branch and wasn't healing well. I often had to go slow because he couldn't keep up with me.

One day when it was cool and cloudy outside in Higginsport, we went for a walk. I had him on his leash, but being tired and slow he just walked calmly beside me. As we passed before a house we had passed many times, I heard the familiar angry bark and growl of a neighborhood German Shepherd. I knew this growl well from my early days of delivering newspapers as a little girl.

The shepherd's yard was surrounded by fence. As we approached, the shepherd was agitated, trotting around nervously and barking nonstop, but still nothing out of the ordinary, so we continued as usual.

In a flash, this German Shepherd for the first time ever cleared the fence and landed in front of us, lunging, barking, and growling at me and Spotty. Spotty wasn't up for this drama so he ran behind me. I knew this wasn't good but had no time to think.

Suddenly, words in a heavenly language known in the Bible as "tongues" came flying out of my mouth with great power and authority. As I spoke, I extended my arm having no idea what I was saying or indicating with that arm, but I was full of faith that the Holy Spirit was giving me unction to speak divine order into our situation.

As I stood there between the two dogs about to be attacked, the Holy Spirit filled my thoughts so that I heard the interpretation of what I had prayed in tongues.

"Go home," I commanded.

I realized that when my arm had extended a moment earlier, it was pointing to the yard next to this shepherd's home.

It all happened so fast.

I spoke the command—not in English, but in the language the Holy Spirit gave to me in that moment.

Immediately, the dog obeyed. His aggression ceased as he took himself right over to the side yard next to his home where I had pointed. Hilariously, he stood there dazed and confused, probably wondering why on earth he was suddenly standing in the neighbor's yard.

Personally, I think the Holy Spirit did that just to make it absolutely clear that I had commanded and the dog obeyed, even when the command didn't make perfect sense to me or to the dog.

I sensed four angels forming a square around me and Spotty with one angel posted at each corner. I couldn't see them, but strongly felt their protective presence, and was filled with total peace. The German Shepherd looked back towards us but acted as if he couldn't even see us anymore.

He was still a little confused, but calm, and I knew his owners would find him there soon. Now that we were safe, Spotty came out from behind me and we continued our walk.

This was one of the last walks I remember with Spotty before the vet had to put him down. He had a growing tumor that was slowly killing him and causing much suffering. I am brought to tears just thinking of how much joy Spotty brought to us every day. God is always with us. He is with us every moment, on every walk, offering His warmth, friendship, comfort, and sometimes—His power and authority to deliver ourselves.

Teacher Bully

When I was in preschool, I mostly enjoyed school and was eager to learn—until I ran into that abusive bully I told you about in chapter one. Everyone was intimidated by her and no one seemed to question her behavior. Most of the time I hadn't the slightest idea why I was getting in trouble with her. Once, I put Oreo cookies in my basket for an afternoon snack. I had never heard that I wasn't allowed to have them, and since Oreos were my favorite thing, I dropped them in and looked forward to eating them. This turned out to be a huge no-no. From out of the blue came Teacher Bully screaming and hollering as she scolded me literally in front of the entire school, leaving me horrified and humiliated.

Another day, I was pulled from the swings during recess.

"You should know better!" she hollered after me as I left the swings. To this day I don't know what I should have known better.

"Hold out your hands," the bully teacher commanded during yet another episode. Over and over she wacked my hands with a wooden paddle. I can almost feel the sting of repeated blows now.

Once, without warning and without explanation, I was taken out through the rain to a separate building to have a bar of soap shoved into my mouth. I was upset and had no idea what was going on. At home I always understood why I was being corrected, which enabled me to learn and adjust my behavior, but I could never figure what I had to do to make this lady happy. What might she suddenly do next time? I don't know what her "disciplining" taught me except to be afraid.

The final straw for me was when an older kid came to drink water in the fountain next to me during nap time. I thought all was well until this kid decided to fill his mouth full of water and spit it all over me. That was it. I had had more than enough from bullies, be it a teacher or student, and I was done!

I got off my mat and headed straight to the teachers' lounge to report what happened. The teachers brought the older boy in to question him, but he lied and said I had stood up during nap time to get a drink from the fountain and got water all over myself. I protested, but they chose to believe the older kid, who received no correction or disciplinary action while I was labeled the liar and troublemaker.

Clearly, there was no teacher nor student nor anyone to help me in this school. All I could do was cry, "I can't take this anymore, God! Please get me out of here!" It was the ugly cry, as Oprah would say.

Sobbing and praying like only a four-year-old could, the peace of God overcame me and I fell asleep.

Only a couple days later my mom showed up in the middle of class to remove my sister and me from the school. She didn't say why, but we never returned. Years later, mom explained that she just had a "gut feeling" with a sense of urgency that we needed to get out of that school. I knew that gut feeling was God.

I felt so free knowing that the mean teacher bully would not be able to mistreat me again. God was real and He had heard my prayer. From that day forward I knew God as my closest Friend and Father. There is nothing He could not or would not do for me.

In case you're wondering, my parents later saved money to put me into a Christian private school where I did well. I never lived in fear there or was treated badly.

I feel very blessed to have experienced God this way at such a young age. If my mom hadn't followed her gut instinct from God, the abuse at school would have continued. Often, God's rescue mission happens through other people. Even in times when it seems there's not a soul around to help, He can and will find a way.

Ants

In my early twenties, when my health was not doing well, it wasn't uncommon for my blood sugar levels to dip so dangerously low that I had to eat every ninety minutes, including through the night. This intensified during or right after an infection, or following large doses of steroid medications for severe allergies and asthma.

In Florida, no matter where you live there will be spiders, ants, or other bugs because of its tropical climate. One night, I was exhausted and fell asleep on the living room couch.

"Laurel, get up," I heard, but shoved it off, preferring to sleep.

Again, "Laurel, get up," and again I rolled over.

Finally, I heard, "Laurel, get up and eat. Your sugar is crashing!"

"God, I'm too cold and tired," I protested, and drifted back to sleep.

This time, God created a new plan. I don't know how He did it, but the next time I awoke it was from sharp stinging on both legs. Ants were biting me!

Finally awake and sitting up because of the pain, I clearly heard the message thundering again: "Get up and eat. Your sugar is crashing!"

I brushed off the ants to check my sugar. It was at 44 and dropping fast.

God is the best Friend ever! He is perfectly willing and able to find creative ways to snatch our attention, and His plans always work so long as we play our part.

I picture what the ants must have heard at this moment:

Beep. Beep. Beep. Line up troops! March into that building. Find the woman on the couch and bite her legs until I say release!

Even the ants obey God and, to be honest, they obey better than I often do. I'm laughing even now thinking of it. Of course, I don't know how God sent the ants. The bites were painful, but God had sent His little ant army to wake me up. They saved my life.

God is so creative. He can use anyone and anything to get our attention and help us. I am blown away by how far He will go to intervene on a daily, moment-to-moment basis. Even in our weaknesses, in our failures, and in our need, He loves us so much.

> *When I remember You on my bed, I meditate and thoughtfully focus on You in the night watches, For You have been my help, and in the shadow of Your wings [where I am always protected] I sing for joy. My soul [my life, my very self] clings to You; Your right hand upholds me.* (Psalm 63:6–8)

Chapter 4

Bobby Pins

*Are not five sparrows sold for two copper
coins? Yet not one of them has [ever] been
forgotten in the presence of God. Indeed the
very hairs of your head are all numbered. Do
not be afraid; you are far more valuable than
many sparrows.* (Luke 12:6–7)

Bobby pins are awesome. I think whoever invented them
should win a Nobel Peace Prize. Maybe that's taking
it too far, but seriously bobby pins are wonderful. I loved
using them in my hair growing up, *and* I had a penchant
for losing them.

At fourteen years old, I did like to be organized, but often
after church or hanging out with friends all I wanted was
to let my hair down and wash off my makeup. Bobby pins
and buttons alike could come flying off me as I made my
way through the house. It was good to be free, but this
often meant that when I needed bobbies for my French
Twist, I couldn't find them.

When I joined the praise and worship ministry at our
church, I took it seriously and still do. Our worship was
like revival in almost every service. I didn't always dress up
but I did usually have my outfit, hair, and makeup laid out
the day before. I loved pulling all of it together because it
was fun!

One Saturday morning, I decided a French Twist would pair excellently with my Sunday outfit. My only challenge with the French Twist was that we worshiped like little wild things with dancing, singing loud, jumping around, and sometimes jumping around a lot. If I didn't use a ton of bobby pins to hold my hair, the few I did have would invariably be tossed out and my hair would be left in a mess. To fulfill my heart's vision and desire for Sunday's dress, I definitely required bobby pins, but with no ride and no license there was no way I could get into town and buy some.

Naturally, therefore, I prayed.

You might think it was silly to ask God for bobby pins, but soon after I prayed, I got a phone call. My friend across the street had a guest who was getting ready for a school dance. She asked whether I might be free to help with hair and makeup, and without hesitation, I said yes.

The young woman brought all kinds of supplies for me to use. I did my very best work for her, as best I could, because with my whole heart I wanted her to look and feel beautiful. Later, she was so pleased with the results that she handed me cash. I was stunned.

"Thank you!" I blurted out.

Then, she said, "You can keep all of my leftover bobby pins, too, if you want? I never use them." With that she handed me her brand-new packs of small and large bobby pins.

I was elated!

God Knows You

This story might seem mild compared to being rescued from drowning or being eaten by a German Shepherd, but it's powerful because it demonstrates His Friendship on another level. God is here with us in every moment. The prayer requests that seem small or mundane are important to Him because they come from you.

On that day, I had a need. In response to my need, God gave me the opportunity to help someone else while expecting nothing at all in return.

In return, He gave me what I needed plus a little extra money!

The whole experience made me so thankful to God. He always does more than we expect, especially when we are generous. He provides not only for our needs, but even blesses us with things we want, which in this case were simple bobby pins. When we remember to encourage others, or when we serve in His church as when leading worship, or opening doors for people, or giving someone a hug if they need one, or anything at all that we do in kindness—God is the kind of Father who rewards you for your service.

There is nothing you could ever do to make God love you more or less. Yet, when you show favor to others, He will show even more favor to you. All we have to do is believe God really is just that good, and don't be afraid to ask. He's a good Daddy who gives good gifts!

Psalm 139 tells us that God formed you in the secret place of your mother's womb. He knows you more intimately than you know yourself—and this is a *good* thing because He sees you not through flaws, but as the perfect child He created. He knows what you love, hate, or long for, and the destiny you were designed to fulfill. He numbers every hair on your head. If you care about your hairstyle, He cares. A great French Twist is not life or death. It's not food, shelter, or even basic survival, but God still thinks and cares about these details because *you* care about them.

Chapter 5

Broken

> *When the righteous cry [for help], the*
> *Lord hears and rescues them from all their*
> *distress and troubles. The Lord is near to*
> *the heartbroken and He saves those who are*
> *crushed in spirit (contrite in heart, truly sorry*
> *for their sin). Many hardships and perplexing*
> *circumstances confront the righteous, but the*
> *Lord rescues him from them all.*
> (Psalm 34:17–19)

Every teenager dreams of the day they can drive a car. It signals that we are moving into new dimensions of freedom and independence. I always took driving seriously and I expected to be a safe driver. I spent a year practicing and attending driver's ed classes before finally earning my license. It was a week before my seventeenth birthday, and I was so excited.

I went to pick up a few companions to go hiking at a nearby park. With no licensed driver to watch out for me and correct me, I was on my own. As I headed to drop a friend at work, everything seemed to be going great *until* I attempted to make a right turn—from the left lane.

In a split second, our lives were forever changed.

The Crash

As I turned right, I cut off the car in the lane next to me. The car smacked the back of our small hatchback Chevette, spinning us at least three revolutions on Highway 52. There was no time to think or react. In a blink, it was over.

"Is everybody alri—" "Where's Grace[1]?" someone blurted out in horror.

Grace had been in the back, and she was gone. As soon I had checked in with everyone still in the vehicle, I went searching.

I found her.

She had been launched to the other side of the highway. The force of us spinning had sucked her out and thrown her under a guard rail, across another two-laned road, and left her tossed in the grass. One of her legs was twisted with the knee facing the opposite direction of her hip. Clearly, her leg was broken. She was in shock and trying to get up.

"Grace!" I stopped her. "Don't move. Your leg is broken and I'm not sure what else could be hurt, so just stay still."

I knew all of this was my fault but had no time to process. I had to focus on Grace and ensuring her survival.

Around this time my friend and sister joined me beside Grace. The driver I had cut off was also a teenager. She was now yelling and cussing me out, which I deserved, but in

---

1   Name has been changed for privacy.

that moment, I couldn't react or respond. I could only stare at Grace and focus on keeping her still. Thankfully, a witness to the accident had already stopped and called 911. I heard myself apologizing to the other driver.

"I didn't see you," I said feebly.

Everyone involved in the accident was under eighteen, so we all had to go to the hospital. It took three ambulances to get us there. Grace was transported first. I waited till she was in good hands, helping her to keep still in case her head or spine were also injured. I focused on her. She was the one who was hurt. She was the one that mattered most. I was the last taken from the scene, put on a backboard and my head taped down into a stabilizer, but I knew I wasn't hurt badly. News crews tried sticking their TV cameras into the back of our ambulance. It was Memorial Day weekend and the media was out looking for accidents involving drunk drivers. The nice older couple running the ambulance told them there was nothing to see here, no drunk drivers, just a teenage accident. They reminded the reporters that we were minors and told them to back off, closing the doors and insulating us from the outside commotion.

As we arrived at the hospital, we were informed that our parents had been notified. Before anyone had arrived, I was visited by a young police officer, probably in his twenties. He informed me that I had made an improper turn and issued me a citation. It turned out that when he was seventeen, he had done the same thing and understood how I felt. I was still in shock, but while laying on that stretcher and backboard talking to the officer—reality began to sink in.

We're all here because of me.

I wondered about Grace.

The ER doctor was kind to assure me that once he took some x-rays and confirmed I was okay, he would take me to see her.

The doctor explained that Grace had a broken leg and was scraped up but that she would be fine. My sister and friend had bumps and bruises, and the other driver had a bump on her head, but only Grace would be staying in the hospital. The rest of us were going home that night. I was so relieved—but then the curtains were pulled back and I saw her lying there.

Now reality hit, and it hit hard.

I immediately burst into sobs, heaving out apologies repeatedly.

"It's okay," she replied. "I'm okay. It was just a mistake."

I blamed myself. All this pain was my fault. Grace was physically broken and torn apart, but my heart was bleeding.

By this time, I was crying uncontrollably. The kind ER doctor seemed to be suffering with us, deep compassion exuding from his face. He left quietly, closing the curtain behind him, lowering his head with tears in his eyes. I didn't see that doctor again after that, but never forgot his kindness. If I saw him today, I would give him a big hug and thank him.

Nurses entered to turn Grace in the bed. I was horrified. Her back was shredded and torn with road rash from being dragged across the highway. Dirt and pebbles were lodged in her skin, some remaining even to this day. Her arms were raw and burning, the flesh exposed. She was in agony.

It was more guilt than I could bear. I knew it was an accident, but I didn't know how to forgive myself. With every passing moment I felt the pounding blows of accusation. People were hurt and it was my fault.

Grace's mom was deeply upset. I was speechless except to whimper, "I'm sorry. It was an accident. I didn't mean for this to happen."

I cried again and sat there allowing her mother to do and say whatever she needed. I knew that my repeated apologies fixed nothing. There was just nothing else I knew to do. I had nothing but a bruised knee, but emotionally I needed open-heart surgery.

Grace was transferred to a major children's hospital in Cincinnati for emergency surgery on her leg, but I couldn't bring myself to go see her right away. I was numb. I was distraught. I felt wrong about not going with my family, but I didn't know how to bear the guilt of seeing her in that state again. I took the day to process and joined on the next visit.

Recovery took months. In that time, Grace needed help with everything. Her mom and family took care of her, and I went to visit when I could. I was glad when she was released home to rest and finish her recovery. I never forgot that their everyday life was drastically changed because of me. My only comfort was knowing everyone was going to be okay in the long run.

I never wanted to drive again.

As time went on, Grace's body continued to heal and re-cover, but I did not.

Nothing in my life has brought more grief to me than this car accident and all of the pain I caused everyone. Many times, I wept before God seemingly unable to release all the guilt I had stored up inside. Sometimes, I couldn't even speak. I just cried and moaned before God in deep grief and discouragement.

When we are broken, He is broken with us. He saw every tear and heard my every cry. God hears you, too. He is ever and always ready to offer us comfort, but it's up to us to receive it.

Freedom

The enemy came in through the door of discouragement, which progressed into self-loathing. I willingly gave Satan, the "accuser," a very real stronghold over my life. I agreed with the lies that I was an awful person unworthy of love. I saw no light nor any end to this tunnel. The discouragement had become entrenched in me, and I carried it everywhere.

I chose to punish myself. I wouldn't let people do nice things for me. Friends at my sister's church wanted to sing me "Happy Birthday" in front of the congregation, but instead I ran out to my car to drive the long country roads alone and weeping. *Why should anyone celebrate my birthday?*

At my cleaning job, the staff got me a gift. It disturbed me so much that I struggled to finish cleaning. *Why are people trying to give me gifts?* I believed that I deserved suffering, grief, and punishment. I refused to receive love or kindness from anyone, including God.

Can God reach us even while we resist Him, fight His goodness, and do our best not to receive His healing?

About a year later, I heard about a Full Gospel Businessmen's Fellowship International Dinner (I know, that's a mouthful) and invited some close friends to join me. This particular evening, the fellowship dinner featured a guest speaker. I did have a slightly sore throat, but other than that I was feeling quite energized and excited to go hear him preach. I'd fixed my hair and makeup and went with great expectancy.

After dinner, we gathered around the speaker. I cannot remember his name or where he was from. I only remember that in the middle of his message, he stopped.

"Someone here is discouraged."

No one responded. I thought to myself, someone must be really hurting for God to stop the message to say this.

The speaker continued.

Again, he stopped.

"Someone here is *really* discouraged."

I was taken aback. It was like watching a TV show and having the news station break in and say, "Breaking news!"

The man continued.

A third time, God interrupted his message.

"Someone here is very discouraged," he repeated with added emphasis. I hoped that whoever it was would be touched by God.

After the message, I felt led by the Holy Spirit to go forward for the altar call and receive prayer. I figured it was for that mild sore throat, but as the speaker began to pray for me, he saw that I was the one being attacked by a spirit of discouragement. He began to pray, and God showed him a picture of an evil spirit sinking its talons deep into my brain.

"I bind that spirit of discouragement," he spoke with rumbling power in his voice, "in the name of Jesus!"

I felt deep pain suddenly uproot. A loud cry came out of me as God seemed to literally pull discouragement all the way from where it started on that day of the crash. Though I was not "possessed" by this evil spirit because of my relationship with Jesus Christ, I had allowed the thing a massive stronghold over me as I came into agreement with its lies.

To answer my earlier question: yes.

Even when we resist, God can find us, reach into the broken places, and in a single moment of willingness, set us free.

I doubled over, sobbing as the man continued to pray for me, "God wants to pick you up and wrap you in a warm blanket of His love."

I felt it as he said it. I was still sobbing, but this time the flow of tears brought healing. This was no mere pat on the back from God. It was an overwhelming sense of His love, acceptance, and encouragement. Only love could remove the root of discouragement planted deep inside—by the power of the name of Jesus.

> *Then the devil left Him; and angels came and ministered to Him [bringing Him food and serving Him].* (Matthew 4:11)

Beloved, no demon can hold you when it is bound by the name of Jesus and you choose to receive God's deliverance. In this world, there is a very real battle between good and evil. Satan and demons come to bring destruction into our lives, but God sends His angels and the Holy Spirit to help us.

Many times, it is good to speak to a godly counselor about the things that have wounded us. Then, there are moments when you just need someone with some discernment who knows Jesus and can pray with power. Writing, speaking, and counseling can all contribute to the healing process, but God is the great Healer and Deliverer. The Bible says that He is near to the broken-hearted and lifts up the lowly. Remember that God is close to you in your time of need.

Dig Deep

Where are you broken? Was it caused by something you have said or done? Did it come from something someone else said or did to you? Did you lose someone you love?

Let's get to the root of our pain and not allow it to steal one more day of our freedom or joy. Ask God to show you if you are broken and why. It may be close to the surface, or it may be buried so deep that you have lost touch with the root issue that started the pain. Let Him, and God will bring restoration and healing to where you are hurting. Cry out to Him and He will hear you. Jesus died so you and I could go straight to God our Father, Creator and Lifelong Friend, not needing a priest or minister because now Christ is your priest and the Holy Spirit is your Comforter. If you have sinned and know what it is, confess that to God and receive His forgiveness without question:

*And Jesus was saying, "Father, forgive them; for they do not know what they are doing." (Luke 23:34)*Staying broken causes us to lash out and hurt people. It causes health problems. It creates negative cycles that will continue until we allow healing to penetrate our wounds. Open your heart today and let Him in. We all need God's open-heart surgery from time to time. Remember, holding on to pain not only hurts you, but will hurt those around you. Let's be real and deal with the things that are eating at us on the inside and not give them a place to hide anymore.

> *"For I know the plans and thoughts that*
> *I have for you," says the* LORD, *"plans for*
> *peace and well-being and not for disaster, to*
> *give you a future and a hope."*
> (Jeremiah 29:11)

Trust God. Believe He wants good things for you. I have found that God wants to restore all areas of brokenness. I even wrote a song about it. After God pulled me out of discouragement and discouragement out of me, He gave me this song:

Humble Child
O Lord, You spoke, and light came to be.
Oh, Jesus, You came and died for me.
By Your blood You have set me free.
Lord, how can it be, in this universe that You see,
I wanna be, Your humble child, Your humble child.
Here passing my days, under Your Son's rays.
Lord, I wanna portray all that You want me to convey.
Lord, I wanna be,
Your humble child, Your humble child.

O Lord, Your awesome might is too great to imagine.
As I sit in my room at night, I will think of Your love's pure height.

Lord, how can it be, in this little child that You see, I
wanna be,
Your humble child, Your humble child.
Here passing my days, under Your Son's rays,
Lord, I wanna portray all that You want me to convey.
Oh, Lord, I am not perfect.
But You receive me anyways.

You wrap me in a warm blanket,
A warm blanket of Your love.
Oh, Lord, I wanna be,
Your humble child.
Here passing my days, under Your Son's rays.
Lord, I wanna portray all that You want me to convey.
Lord, I wanna be,
Your humble child, Your humble child.

Chapter 6

Facing Epilepsy

> *He was despised and rejected by men, a Man*
> *of sorrows and pain and acquainted with*
> *grief; and like One from whom men hide*
> *their faces He was despised, and we did not*
> *appreciate His worth or esteem Him.*
> (Isaiah 53:3)

In the blink of an eye, everything can change. God can heal you, change your circumstances, or save you from driving off a cliff on the icy 221.

Sometimes, He does that.

Other times, we walk through challenging seasons that don't end right away.

Suffering

Jesus is the "man of sorrows" who was "acquainted with grief" in Isaiah 53:3. He did nothing but love, serve, heal, deliver, and teach; yet, He was rejected, violently pursued, and eventually beaten till unrecognizable, stripped naked and shamed, and murdered slowly on an instrument of torture called a cross.

> *For we do not have a High Priest who is*
> *unable to sympathize and understand our*
> *weaknesses and temptations, but One who*

> *has been tempted **[knowing exactly how it***
> ***feels to be human]** in every respect as we are,*
> *yet without [committing any] sin.*
>   (Hebrews 4:15, emphasis mine)

Nothing that happens to us is meaningless.

Christ's sufferings assure us that He understands our condition in this broken world and knows how to heal us, but also that God can take even the most treacherous act of murder and turn it into the greatest blessing in human history—eternal forgiveness and everlasting life. In that one act, God proved that He can and will use anything, even the worst atrocities we may have suffered, and turn them all for good. We just have to let Him.

> *…[with joy] let us exult in our*
> *sufferings and rejoice in our hardships,*
> *knowing that hardship (distress, pressure,*
> *trouble) produces patient endurance; and*
> *endurance, proven character (spiritual*
> *maturity); and proven character,*
> *hope and confident assurance [of eternal*
> *salvation].*   (Romans 5:3–4)

Our hardships make us stronger. Our sufferings allow us to relate to one another and grow in compassion to comfort others through their trials.

Jesus said:

> *The thief comes only in order to steal and kill*
> *and destroy. I came that they may have life,*

and have it in abundance [to the full, till it
overflows].　　　　　　　　　　(John 10:10)

Regardless of what trials you may experience, God is the one who always loves us, fights for us, heals us, and carries us as we choose to live for Him and with Him.

Seizures

I will never forget the day I realized I had epilepsy. At that time, everything seemed great. I had three jobs: cleaning houses, babysitting, and caretaking as a certified nursing assistant. My long days of caretaking followed by three hours of roundtrip driving to and from the city had taken a heavy toll on my health, so I had just cut my caretaking hours and was enjoying a little more downtime and rest. Things were looking up.

On this particular day, I came home excited because my client's wife had given her life to the Lord. This couple had become like family to me. She was elderly and struggling to care for her husband. Though a Roman Catholic for many years, until that day she didn't understand that she could be in a personal relationship with Jesus. I always prayed with her before I left, but this day she connected with God herself and understood that He heard her prayers.

It was February of 2000 and cool outside in Higginsport, Ohio, with no indication that it would be my last day of normalcy for a long time to come.

I returned home from work around noon to finish packing before my dad and I would leave to get Mom. It was vacation time, and we were driving to Florida for a full week. I bounced around like a small child on Christmas as I threw my things into the Blazer, enjoying the brisk winter air as we prepared to leave for the warm Sunshine State.

During the drive to get Mom from work, I was talking to my dad when my left arm suddenly flew overhead. Simultaneously, my speech became slurred and confused. Epilepsy runs in our family. I knew instantly.

"Dad," I said, shocked, "I think I just had a seizure."

We stayed calm. Mom was shocked, too, and wondered whether we should do something about it, but afterwards I seemed fine; so, we continued our long drive towards vacation.

When we stopped to eat, I had no appetite and my head felt strange. Later in the car, I got nauseous. Soon after, I started seeing double. The white line on the right side of the road seemed to be moving in toward the left. I became lightheaded and dizzy, which I later found out is a symptom called "seizure auras," which let you know a seizure may be oncoming. I assumed it would subside.

We stopped at a hotel for the night and everyone fell right asleep. I remember awaking in the night for just a few seconds, my body hot and drenched in sweat, and then must have drifted back to sleep.

In the morning, my head still felt strange. My body did not feel rested but weak and tired. My mouth tasted weird. Smiling in the mirror, dried blood was crusted on my teeth.

I spit into the sink. Old blood splattered the white basin. I rinsed my mouth and brushed my teeth, trying to wash out all the dried blood. My tongue and gums were cut. Even the gums in the back of my mouth were torn from my own teeth, so I knew it must have been a bad one.

Standing in the shower, I accepted that something was wrong and we could no longer ignore it, but what could we do now? In the days following I continued to experience sudden jerks or jolts that often affected my whole body, but we were far from home, we didn't have health insurance, and we were already halfway to our destination. We decided to see a doctor after the trip. Nothing would keep us from this vacation.

Driving home to Ohio, I was resting in the front seat, sunlight flashing through the trees and mountains as we drove. It was brighter than usual because of the snow. I shut my eyes.

Suddenly, I felt myself losing control. I couldn't breathe normally or open my eyes. I felt my body shake.

"Keep your eyes open," my dad warned, hoping the flashing light wouldn't bother me as much. I managed to pry my eyelids apart.

A Cocktail of Drugs

My doctor put me on an anti-seizure medication called Depakote and ordered me a CAT scan. He was concerned I might have a brain tumor because I didn't have seizures as a child, and I was now twenty. I told him four other people in our family have epilepsy, including my father. I was sure this was hereditary and not a tumor.

About a week after I started the Depakote, I remember being at church on a Sunday morning. Again came seizure auras, my head feeling strange and a little dizzy. I grew cold and pale.

"Are you alright?" someone asked.

"I'm just cold, is all." I was still new to the symptoms.

During the announcements, everything suddenly became still and quiet. What happened next, I don't remember. When I awoke, I was on the shoulder of the person next to me and could hear people calling my name. Slowly I regained consciousness. My left hand twitched and jerked mildly. People were still talking to me. A few church members helped me out of the sanctuary and got me to the hospital. I was able to walk inside, but I quickly felt weak again.

For the next six days in the hospital doctors tried to figure out which dose of Depakote I could tolerate. They ordered me an electroencephalogram (EEG) and a few hours later I had a tonic-   clonic seizure, which is also known as a grand mal seizure, the type that causes loss of consciousness and stiffness or violent muscle contractions.

You didn't need medical training to know this was bad. I shared the hospital room with a lady who was staying with her ill mother. Every time I had a seizure, my roommate would check the time and then run to get the nurses.

Apparently, this one carried on for fifteen minutes before nurses or staff came to my aid.

That evening, it happened again.

The kind woman in my room glanced at her watch and ran for help.

This time, the nurses did come to my side but insisted that I was faking it. I think my brain was trying to come out of it because fifteen minutes into the seizure, I remember for just a second my eyes opened and then quickly shut. I could no longer see, nor could I move or speak, but I could hear.

"Laurel," said a male voice, "we know you are faking it, so you might as well stop!"

I was unable to respond because I was *not* faking it. The last thing I remember before I completely blacked out was someone holding my eyes open and shining light into them.

"This is real," he said. "Run! Go get the medicine out of the fridge."

I blacked out and went back into a seizure, not regaining consciousness until the middle of the night, soaked in sweat. My roomie told me it took the nurses twenty-five minutes to figure out it was real.

The following morning, I was able to speak with the male nurse who said I was faking it until he checked my eyes.

My EEG came back abnormal, which was comforting in a strange way. I knew they needed to see it on an EEG to give me the full diagnosis. He explained that nurses see a lot of people faking seizures to get drugs. I told him I am not ever faking it, and this runs in my family. These were extremely dangerous seizures because they went on for long periods of time with the potential to cause brain damage and even death. Most hospitals cannot monitor a seizure patient closely enough, so if you know someone being hospitalized with seizures, it is best to keep them with someone who knows them well in case of a serious problem.

After speaking with the nurse, I was glad to put it behind me. Hearing that I was faking it when I could not speak or even open my eyes taxed me emotionally. I longed to rest and recover.

Prior to my release, the doctor accidentally gave me too much Depakote. Increasing from 500 mg to 1,000 mg, I went into toxic overdose.

During these difficult times I tried to stay positive and continued to talk to God. I prayed for Him to heal me and give me the strength I needed to face epilepsy.

A local neurologist found I was having too many different types of seizures for him to sort out and treat, so a year after the seizures first began, I was sent to see a neurologist specializing in epilepsy (epileptologist) at the University of Cincinnati.

They took me off the anti-seizure medication and put me on a twenty-four-hour EEG and EKG. I was also on constant audio and visual monitoring except while in the bathroom. To test what would happen if I was sleep deprived, I was only allowed to sleep from 3:00 a.m. to 7:00 a.m. the first two nights.

They found out real quick! During my four-day stay, I had fifty-five myoclonic seizures. Most of them were observed during the first two days. After that, we started Depakote intravenously.

The specialist determined that what I had was, in fact, hereditary, and officially diagnosed me with Juvenile Myoclonic Epilepsy. Myoclonic seizures can be mild or severe jolts or jerk-like movements and can even throw you backwards or down to the ground. That happened to me once. I was heading to the bathroom when it happened suddenly and a nurse caught me. Therefore, I had to be accompanied by a nurse or physician whenever upright and walking.

The test results showed I had a lot of brain defects. My IQ score was around 85. I am not good at those tests, but I did score high in one area. They said I have a "superior delayed audible memory." I could recall almost every detail of a story read aloud after a passage of time. Recall was excellent five minutes later, but more details were remembered as time passed. I was glad to learn that at least one part of my brain was not considered defective, or what they call "borderline" defective. The neuropsychologists in the unit didn't think I would have been smart enough to get through high school with an IQ so low, but I told them I studied and worked hard and had good grades. Before I could graduate, I had become too sick with fevers and sinus infections to finish, but passed my GED exam at nineteen and also became a certified nursing assistant.

A few rough years and fourteen anti-seizure medications later, I was blessed to find a wonderful neurologist at a Florida facility called Shands. I was scared and nervous when I met this doctor because so many doctors and professionals had judged me. I had nearly died from an ER doctor pulling me off Ativan cold. He didn't believe I was on the drug for seizures and refused to confirm it with my neurologist. Ativan is not an everyday anti-seizure medication, but after having serious problems with over fourteen other meds, it was my neurologist's last resort. Doctors who don't know your history, such as those in the ER, can make dangerous snap decisions. I didn't know what to expect, but I put my trust in God that He would help me find the right physician.

I will never forget how I broke down when this new neurologist mentioned another medication to try. The trauma from my body's reactions to the wrong meds was almost worse than the seizures themselves. Seeing that I was distraught, the neurologist told me about a study he was conducting on a new epilepsy treatment. It was no more or less than a simple packet of electrolytes added to water. I happened to tell him that for some reason when I was on prednisone for asthma, the seizures would completely stop. He couldn't say for sure but saw a correlation as the steroid drug does increase absorption of sodium, which is an electrolyte. Light bulb!

He made no promises but invited me to participate in the electrolyte study.

"It will work," I said. "I know it will!"

I was given the electrolytes plus 400 mg daily of magnesium oxide. It worked! However, the high doses of sodium and potassium didn't sit well with my right kidney, and I was sent to yet another specialist. It turned out that my kidney had been damaged from anti-seizure medications, but we didn't know that until we pushed it with high levels of electrolytes. The electrolytes did in fact help to stabilize me, but I had to stop the treatment to avoid losing kidney function.

Many years later, I learned about magnesium chloride.

The Spa Wins

Now, to remain stable and seizure-free, I don't take toxic medications. I don't stay in hospitals. I soak in a bath of Ancient Minerals magnesium chloride, a simple protocol given to me by triple board-certified doctor, scientist, and researcher, Dr. Zach Bush.

In addition to seizures, Dr. Bush had noticed that I was having pronounced dysautonomia, a condition that causes disfunction to the autonomic nervous system potentially affecting the heart, bladder, intestines, sweat glands, pupils, and blood vessels. Before the magnesium treatment, I had trouble regulating body temperature. On the one hand, I would perspire while in a perfectly cool room for no apparent reason. On the other hand, my body could become hot but barely sweat and have trouble cooling down. Once, I was on a plane that had overheated. Then, *I* overheated and was unable to cool off for hours. This problem had me in a state of chronic dehydration. I often had dried-out, chunky-looking lips before implementing the bath remedy, but the treatment also helped my body to sweat properly.

Dr. Bush prescribed a handful of all-natural treatments for root cause support and to reset my nervous system. Treatments included Egoscue Therapy, acupuncture, chiropractic treatments, and intravenous magnesium to handle dysautonomia flare ups.

It was great, but a month later when no one was available to administer the magnesium IV and I was having seizures, dysautonomia, and dystonia, he instructed me to soak in a minimum ten pounds of Ancient Minerals magnesium chloride bath flakes.

I did this for three days straight.

Both the seizures and other neurological symptoms stopped almost entirely. I also had an Ancient Minerals magnesium chloride oil to spray on my feet before bed to help prevent night seizures. To this day, twice per week I soak in seven to eight pounds; or, in a crisis, ten or more pounds of the magnesium chloride.

Typically, now that things are calm, I use the oil on the days I haven't soaked in the magnesium bath. If I get dehydrated or have high stress, or if I exercise, I have to soak in the magnesium baths more frequently.

Ancient Minerals magnesium comes from a clean ocean and is further purified so it contains no heavy metals or toxins. I am forever grateful to have found a treatment from nature I can tolerate without negative side effects. It also helps everything else in my body work more normally.

It may sound too good to be true, but it really works. Most doctors are not aware of magnesium as a treatment that can alleviate so many serious health conditions. My neurologist is still amazed. In over seven years, he had never seen me so stable.

I am amazed, too, at how God uses simple things like electrolytes in a spa treatment to calm the neurological storms raging in my body.

God does answer our prayers and brings us exactly what we need. We just need to remain open and watch for what He shows us about our health along the way. If I believed the only way God could heal was to supernaturally deliver me from a spirit of infirmity, I would still have certain health problems. For what I needed, manmade drugs failed, but God had a natural solution. He had already provided magnesium in the earth, and He led me right to it. I just had to be willing to try!

I once had seizures nearly every day and night. I will never forget what it felt like to lose control of my body. I thank God for how far He has brought me. I've held this Scripture close to my heart during these twenty years of health battles:

And he went through all Galilee, teaching in their synagogues and preaching the good news (gospel) of the kingdom, and **healing every kind of disease and every kind of sickness among the people** *[demonstrating and revealing that He was indeed the promised Messiah].*

So, the news about him spread throughout all of Syria; and they brought to Him all who were sick ... **and He healed them.**
(Matthew 4:23–24, emphasis mine)

Let me encourage you in what God reminds me often. Have a few Scriptures that you hold in your heart to strengthen your fight of faith. Never speak death over yourself, saying things like, "I will never be well," or, "Nothing good ever happens to me." God created us and all the creation by speaking. Your voice and your words carry power. Instead of being discouraged and downtrodden, I speak life over my body. I speak life over my mind. I speak life over my finances

Chapter 7

Wolf in Sheep's Clothing

*Be sober [well balanced and self-disciplined],
be alert and cautious always. That enemy of
yours, the devil, prowls around like a roaring
lion [fiercely hungry], seeking someone to
devour.* (1 Peter 5:8)

I was broken before Wolf[2] found me.

The very first rape was the worst, in a way, because I was twenty-two years old and had protected my virginity, committed to keeping myself pure for God. It happened in the fall just before meeting Wolf.

I had lost my virginity to a sexual predator from a cousin's church. He was mild compared to Wolf, but the first time I was raped broke me like I did not know I could break. I felt numb and empty, dead and lifeless inside.

I called to tell a close friend what happened. He lived far away, but he told my younger sister. She and a friend dropped everything and drove all the way from Ohio to get me from Florida. I am very thankful to the friend who called my sister, and for her sacrifice to get me out of harm's way. My health was still shaky, but at least there were no predators at my sister's house in Ohio. Over the years, many people have gone out of their way to help me

---

2   To protect his identity, the man in this chapter is noted as "Wolf," which is fitting.

and I am incredibly grateful to each person. They were truly kind to me.

I knew that dealing with my health challenges and seizures was eventually going to be too much for my sister and brother-in-law. I can always tell when people need a break. I was having seizures night and day, and no one can really handle all of this for long. After living with them for a few months, I returned to Florida and couch-surfed, mostly staying with a cousin and occasionally with my grandparents in their small apartment.

I still needed a lot of help with food, rides to medical appointments, picking up medications, and sometimes trips to the ER.

l was living just to survive.

My grandma had wanted me to stay with her where she could keep an eye on me and keep me safe, but my grandpa told me to stay away. He called me a drug addict, saying I was too much of a burden and was not welcome on their property. He didn't want Grandma worrying or driving me anywhere.

I stayed away from them as much as possible.

A year later, my grandpa and I became close again. He admitted that he did not understand what I was going through until he needed cancer treatments that made him feel awful. He apologized and totally changed the way he was treating me. He was just trying to survive, too.

Before Grandpa passed, I told him about how God had been with me throughout my life as my friend and what He had brought me through. My grandpa encouraged me to write this book so people would know what kind of friend God really is to us.

Zip-Tied

Wolves are predators by nature. In my case, it felt like I was the primary food source.

He was a few years older and seemed pretty put-together. We met at the Messianic Jewish synagogue. He was a worship leader and deeply loved. Perhaps like many wolves in sheep's clothing, he was the type of guy who loved to help. He'd be the first one to show up on your move day to help you get your furniture loaded. He volunteered often and liked for people to see him in this light. Second Corinthians 11:14–15 tell us:

> *Satan himself masquerades as an angel of*
> *light. So, it is no great surprise if his servants*
> *masquerade as servants of righteousness, but*
> *their end will correspond with their deeds.*

Being so highly favored by others at the synagogue, I believed it would be safe to date him. Surely, if something were crazy wrong with him, someone would have stopped him from leading worship and volunteering, right?

Wrong.

Although the people around me were fooled, God my protector was putting up red flags everywhere. Sadly, sometimes we are weak and don't act on His warnings. This is exactly what happened to me. I saw red flags from the very first time Wolf put his hand on my shoulder. I felt uncomfortable, but assumed it was just trauma from the rape. I always assumed the problem was with me.

The week we started dating, my doctor decided he had no choice but to put me back on Ativan three times per day to help control the seizures. Ativan changed the very fabric of my personality. On it I was introverted, quiet, afraid to speak, and more likely to go with the flow. I was often drowsy, forgetful, and had trouble focusing through the thick fog it seemed to cause in my brain. Because of the complications with Depakote, which aggravated my liver, I was weighing in at about ninety-four to ninety-six pounds. It caused much of my hair to fall out and left me with severe reflux, nausea, and resultant weight loss. The Ativan affected me badly, too, but I tolerated it better than Depakote, and it was the best my neurologist felt he could do. I was twenty-two, underweight, and often drowsy and weak.

Wolf had medical training as an EMT and was in nursing school studying to become an RN, so he had more knowledge about the medical battles I faced than most guys I knew. He seemed like the good shepherd coming to help an injured sheep.

Being so sick and struggling just to survive made me an easy target. Wolf showed up as kind and generous, outgoing and happy. Why wouldn't I date this man? He took me out to dinner. We went go-karting and did fun things. He also began bringing me to his home.

At the time, we were just hanging out. *No big deal*, I thought. Another red flag was ignored.

Because of my condition and my body's reaction to the meds, I needed rides just to get to the doctor, pick up medication, buy groceries—I was depending on help for everything, and Wolf started coming to my rescue.

When he started to get too physical, still pushing himself on me despite my protests, I ignored the warning sign and told myself he would eventually listen and back off.

I should have ended it there.

He wasn't seeking a relationship, but I didn't see that until it was too late.

Being on Ativan made it easy to break my will. I did not want to have sex, but Wolf eventually wore me down. He was like a hungry animal always on the prowl to feed his insatiable appetite for sex and control. It took me a while to realize I had been hunted and was being eaten alive.

With the Ativan in my system every eight hours, I had little time to think clearly between doses, except this one evening. I knocked on Wolf's bedroom door, asking him to take me home.

No reply.

Home would have been my grandparents' house where I was not exactly welcome, but I was feeling unsafe and like I had to get out.

Again, I knocked.

Still no reply.

Every few minutes, I knocked and asked again, but he would not come out or even respond. Finally, I took a full basket of clean laundry I had folded and threw the whole thing at his door and said, "I want to go home!" I was sure I said it loud enough this time.

Finally, Wolf reluctantly emerged. By this time, it was around 9:30 or 10:00 p.m. I had felt frustrated, angry, and trapped.

"You're out of control!" he hollered at me.

"I just want to go home!" I cried.

He walked out to his silver Dodge Ram pickup truck. When he returned, he moved toward me holding zip ties. I tried to get away. He grabbed me and shoved my hands behind my back.

"Let me go!" I squirmed and tried pulling away, but as I was yelling, he zip-tied my wrists together so tightly I couldn't move them. As I tried fighting and yelling, he pushed me down and tied my ankles together.

I forced my head sideways so I could breathe. Attempting to drag myself across the decades-old brownish carpet to put distance between us, he quickly grabbed my already bound ankles and wrists and zip-tied them together.

It all happened so fast. I was in shock. Tears flowed like a waterfall down my cheeks. I felt pressure in my head. I tried struggling to no avail. I was in bondage.

Wolf turned off the living room lights, walked across the room, and started blasting heavy metal. I just laid there, crying, not sure what to do next or how long I'd be stuck in this painful position, hog-tied like a piece of meat. The music was so loud it pumped through my ears and whole body. I thought for sure the neighbors would come and complain, but no one came. I couldn't run. I couldn't walk. I couldn't even stand up because of the way he had me tied. No matter how much noise I made, or how hard I tried to escape, I was going to be bound until he chose to release me. Worn out and tired, I just lay there on the floor waiting.

Two hours later, he came back to ask, "Are you ready to behave now?"

Knowing it was the only way I would be loosed from the zip ties, I said yes. He believed me. I felt pressure against my ankles and wrists as he began removing the ties. Finally, I could breathe.

"I just want to go home," I told him.

In a calm voice, he replied, "Not tonight. I'm too tired. Take your Ativan and go to sleep on the couch."

It was about midnight. I had missed my night dose of Ativan, so I took it and tried to go to sleep but my mind was spinning. Here I was, a twenty-two-year-old young woman disabled from seizures and other health problems, just trying to figure out a way to survive, and I found myself in a terrible relationship with a sick abusive man.

How did I wind up here?

I really needed 24/7 care, but there was no one in my life willing or able to do that. Sometimes I made the right choices and sometimes I didn't, but as a couch-surfer trying my best not to overburden my friends and family, my choices were often based on where I might get the most rest for a few days. At no time did I want to be in this bad relationship. He didn't have the right to control, manipulate, and abuse me. My Lifelong Friend is the exact opposite. He never ties me up or tries to control me. He gives me choices and stands ready to help whenever I call on Him. Even in this dark moment when I felt like I was a failure and ashamed, God had never left me.

In time, Wolf had gained almost full power over me. He took over as my main caregiver in many ways, but this was a front so that he could control me. When I slept, ate, did chores, swam in his pool, went to the grocery store, or did anything at all, I was instructed what to say, and often told to try and look "okay" even if I felt faintish from the ongoing health battles. I did not mind helping around the house at first, but that became another area of slavery. I had to do work around his house even if I was not well or needed to rest. How else would I earn my keep?

I tried to be independent but it was a futile exercise. Soon after the zip-tie incident, Wolf began raping me regularly. Sometimes I was raped two to three times in a day. He was a sex addict who needed a fix every few hours. To my knowledge, he didn't drink much or take drugs. Control and orgasms were his drugs of choice.

Sometimes after raping me, he would say, "If I confess my sins, God will cleanse me from all unrighteousness." So, he thought, raping is okay if you occasionally confess it.

Dangers of Porn

Wolf told me that his problems with pornography started when he was young. He was raised mostly by his father and seemed to lack respect for certain women. I must have fit the bill, because he thought it was totally fine to do whatever he wanted with me. Before long, every area of my life was controlled by him.

Sometimes, I tried to be helpful because part of him seemed kind, and the caregiver in me wanted to see him healed and doing well. I thought maybe if I could help him, he might change and leave the pornography and sex addictions for good, but having me in his life made his weaknesses worse.

To this day, I don't even know all of what he did to me. On at least one occasion he drugged me. I woke up in his room naked on his bed. He seemed calm and satisfied and left me alone but would not tell me what happened. I can only remember waking up naked, groggy, and confused, but knowing something was wrong.

As his addiction worsened, he would cancel meetings with clients to rape me or masturbate watching porn.

"I got stuck in traffic and I am going to be late today," he frequently lied. "Unless you would prefer to reschedule?"

Clients often rescheduled, giving him more time to rape me. I had become Wolf's literal sex slave. One evening, I accidentally walked into the living room while he was watching porn and gratifying himself. I almost physically threw up.

I know watching pornography is not a criminal act, but feeding that addiction led to rape, which is 100 percent criminal. Porn is a real addiction many people face and it's promoting real harm to boys, girls, teens, women, and the disabled.

I was often too weary and unstable from seizures, weakness, and health battles to wear anything special or dress up, but he would force me to put on makeup and do my hair to pretend I was healthy and doing just fine.

Every part of me just broke—body, soul, mind, and spirit.

Sometimes I would build up the strength and courage to leave. As he saw what I was doing, he would taunt me, "I hope you can get to your doctor's appointment tomorrow," reminding me that I had no money, rides, or even the ability to work. I felt trapped.

Jesus said:

> *You have heard that it was said, "YOU*
> *SHALL LOVE YOUR NEIGHBOR (fellow*
> *man) and hate your enemy."*
>
> *But I say to you, **love** [that is unselfishly seek*
> *the best or higher good for] **your enemies** and*
> *pray for those who persecute you....*
>
> *For if you love [only] those who love you,*
> *what reward do you have? Do not even the*
> *tax collectors do that?*
> (Matthew 5:43–44, 46, emphasis mine)

It was many months before I felt I could pray for Wolf, but when I did, I felt God healing me inside. For one thing, it's hard to pray for someone else's freedom and simultaneously remain bitter towards them. He still wasn't treating me right, but praying for him helped me to forgive, and forgiving him helped me to focus on escaping. To be honest, the more difficult task was forgiving myself.

How did I get myself into this? Why is it so hard to get away?

Chapter 8

Wanted

*…whatever is pure and wholesome, whatever
is lovely and brings peace, whatever is
admirable and of good repute; if there is
any excellence, if there is anything worthy
of praise, think continually on these things
[center your mind on them, and implant them
in your heart].* (Philippians 4:8)

Disgusted with myself for living with a man who only
wanted to use me for sex and control, I left the house
late one night just to get out. In my mind, it was better to
wander the streets alone in the dark than wait for Wolf to
come home and abuse me.

Maybe I would be better off living out here than with him.

I deeply considered it.

I was frustrated with how helpless I had become. I hated
my life. I hated myself for getting trapped inside it. I was
beyond damaged. I was a walking disaster.

Things couldn't be any worse out here on the streets, could they?

Maybe things would be worse out there, but I thought
it might be worth a try. At least I'd be doing something
different. Perhaps this was irrational thinking, but no less
rational than staying with a man who was raping me daily
and controlling every area of my life.

Still, I felt there was no one on earth who could feasibly take his place. Only a handful of people loved, accepted, and wanted me, and they were unable to provide the level of care and help I needed. I felt like some sort of freak because of seizures. People often avoided me like I had leprosy. There are not many things in life that are more painful than feeling unwanted almost everywhere you go.

"God," I prayed an aching prayer, "Who wants me? Where do I belong? Where can I go and stay? What should I—""Are you crazy!"

Wolf's voice pierced my prayer and scattered my thoughts.

"It's not safe to be out walking around by yourself at night!"

It's not safe to be with you either, I thought.

Reluctantly, I climbed into his truck.

I felt even God didn't want me, and if God didn't want me, then what reason did I have to keep on living? Certainly not this wonderful life I currently endured. I couldn't go back to my dad in Ohio. For one thing, the house was in an unlivable condition as he was busy with renovations and repairs, while simultaneously dealing with a tenant who was beyond awful. Plus, he would have had to drive me to the city constantly just to make my appointments. I knew it was too much to ask of him.

My mom was taking care of her mother and other elderly relatives in another city. My younger sister and brother-in-law had already taken me in for a few months and I knew they needed a break. My grandma wanted to help, but she didn't know Grandpa had told me to stay away. My cousin and her husband took me in many times to live with them, but they had a lot going on and she was pregnant. The only one who could *sort of* handle me was the rapist boyfriend who needed me to act out his sexual fantasies and addictions in turn for his "care."

What about staying at a shelter? I wondered.

That's a great idea! I told myself, so I looked into it.

I found out there was no shelter or transitional housing for someone like me. You can't stay in a shelter if you have epilepsy, and my prescription medications would have made me a target for robbery as people use them to get high.

I am sure I could have gotten more help if I had found a way to speak up about what was happening, but I really didn't know how to talk about the mess that had become my life. Most of the time the abuse was in a room with a locked door and I rarely opened that door to anyone. God was always there sending me guidance and encouragement, but I made the mistake of believing Satan's lies that I was unwanted and unworthy. Agreeing with Satan is always dangerous. It only leads to death and destruction.

If you believe lies and rehearse them in your mind, you become deaf to the truth. If you believe that God is not for you, you won't hear His cry calling you. If He tells you He loves you, you won't believe Him. If you hear His guidance, you'll reject it. You'll believe the lie and forsake the truth.

The truth was and is that God always wanted me. He always loved and accepted me. He never judged me but wanted to heal me and take me to a safe place. I just needed to let Him.

> *You are my hiding place; You, L*ORD *, protect*
> *me from trouble; You surround me with*
> *songs and shouts of deliverance. Selah.*
>
> (Psalm 32:7)

Chapter 9

The Suicide Cloud

> *My soul has been cast far away from peace;*
> *I have forgotten happiness. So, I say, "My*
> *strength has perished and so has my hope*
> *and expectation from the LORD." ...But this*
> *I call to mind; therefore, I have hope. It is*
> *because of the LORD's loving kindnesses that*
> *we are not consumed, because **His [tender]***
> ***compassions never fail. They are new every***
> ***morning; great and beyond measure is Your***
> ***faithfulness.***
>
> (Lamentations 3:17–18, 21–23,
> emphasis mine)

I was rapidly losing hope. I now took Ativan three to four times daily on top of other toxic medications, yet never getting any better. I was needy and felt unwanted. I grew convinced that even God had given up on me, and I knew I could never be smart or strong enough to make it on my own. I couldn't even manage to run away from the man who was abusing me.

Day after day, like a broken record, I heard the voice of Satan in my head.

"You've gone too far," he'd say. "No one wants you. Even God has abandoned you."

Hearing this lie for months on end, nearly 24/7, I eventually accepted it as true.

"You're going to hell anyway," I heard hour after hour, "so you might as well just end it."

This sounds crazy for anyone who actually knows God. I knew better than that. I knew I could never run far enough or get into so much trouble that God would stop loving me. I knew I wasn't too much for God. I knew I could never go so far in sin and bad choices that He couldn't reach me. Scripture assures us of this:

> *If I ascend to heaven, You are there;*
>
> *If I make my bed in Sheol (the nether world, the place of the dead), behold, You are there.*
>
> *If I take the wings of the dawn,*
>
> *If I dwell in the remotest part of the sea,*
>
> *Even there Your hand will lead me, and Your right hand will take hold of me.*
> (Psalm 139:8–10)

His mercy is new every morning and great is His faithfulness.

I needed to tell myself that. I needed to remind myself, or let someone else who knew God remind me, but those weren't the words I chose to meditate upon day and night.

I tried fighting the suicide cloud that followed me constantly, but I was growing weaker by the second. Listening to Satan's lies, I became convinced my life was a waste. I looked at my circumstances and was further persuaded.

Satan was right … *right?*

No, Satan can never be right. Jesus made that clear when He said of the devil:

> *He was a murderer from the beginning, and does not stand in the truth because **there is no truth in him.***
>
> *When he lies, he speaks what is natural to him, for he is a liar and the father of lies and half-truths.* (John 8:44)

The mind-altering medications made it harder for me to focus on much of anything, including God and His Word. Satan exploited the drug's effects coupled with my weaknesses to erode the strong foundation of God's lifelong friendship and love.

I felt guilty. I felt ashamed. I felt nasty and dirty inside. I was confused. Even worse, part of me cared about the man who was hurting me. There's a name for that. It's called Stockholm Syndrome. I wanted to believe that in some twisted way his behaviors exhibited real love.

But if he loves me, why would he hurt me?

"Love does no harm," the Scripture says in Romans 13:10.

I was harmed just by having sex with a man who was not my husband. It wasn't what I wanted. It wasn't the true me. It was sin. Sin harms us, so God warns us to flee from it. I wanted to flee from it. I wanted to be free of it, but I had given up and given in.

I don't say the Ativan medication was stronger than God, but it weakened me greatly. I felt like I couldn't see through the fog of drowsiness and woes. I became convinced this was the sin for which God could not forgive me. I stopped believing that the blood of Jesus was enough to make me clean.

Satan always wants you to believe that Jesus's blood is insufficient. It's Satan who says you must suffer and work tirelessly to become worthy of God's mercy.

The truth is that Jesus's blood is more than enough for anything anyone has ever done. If you don't believe me, consider that while He was dying on the cross, Jesus said to His Father in heaven concerning His murderers:

> *Father, forgive them; for they do not know*
> *what they are doing.*   (Luke 23:34)

We killed God, and God answered us by healing us. On the cross, Christ nailed every accusation against you and buried it in the tomb with His dead body. When He resurrected and ascended, He became the promise of total forgiveness and new life for all who choose to receive and follow Him as their Lord and Savior. Confess your sins to Jesus. He's not mad. Confession just helps you come clean and let go so you can receive the forgiveness He already gave you two thousand years ago. Then, you can look to Him all day, every day to guide you and give you wisdom. He will pour out grace and power to turn away from addictions, fear, and everything that harms you so you can live in His freedom.

Jesus Himself said that all we need do to enjoy this freedom is to believe, but I allowed myself to doubt.

Would anyone even understand that I was being raped even though I "chose" to be in this relationship? Why couldn't I just leave for good and stay away from him? I wondered what was wrong with me and concluded that I was defective—too timid on the one hand, and overly talkative on the other, driving people away even more.

I didn't fit. I didn't belong even with my family.

Mentally, emotionally, and spiritually I felt cut at every possible angle, bleeding out from all my battle wounds like a bloody scene from the movie *Braveheart*.

I feared telling anyone how I was thinking lest I end up in a psych ward, where they would never believe I was on Ativan for seizures. If I risked it and spoke with someone, they might call me a drug addict or pull me off my meds cold as in times past, injuring or possibly even killing me.

Everyone I knew had their own problems. I wanted to work, but couldn't. Driving was not an option at all. I was defective and there was no one and nothing left that could fix me.

True—had I known God was still rooting for me, that He was on my side and still had plans and a purpose for me, I could press through this whole mess and go on; but day after day I was bombarded with suicidal thoughts.

Where is God? Why isn't His voice the one that stands out in my mind?

Only the dark thoughts prevailed, and I couldn't stop the broken record. I was too isolated. People don't usually commit suicide in front of people. They isolate, then carry out their plan. The suicide cloud had hung around for months. Up until this moment, I had hope, but that was all gone. I was ready to take control. Standing in Wolf's dining room, I decided to end it all. Never again could he come home and rape me. No more would I burden everyone around me with my battles just to survive. Everything was my fault— everything. I felt like no one wanted me, like even God no longer wanted me.

I can see now that God was still present with me in those dark moments, but that afternoon, my head was too filled and racing with dark thoughts.

I had already taken my 1 mg morning dose of Ativan as prescribed. When it came time for my afternoon dose, I grabbed my bottle of Ativan, the very drug that was supposed to keep me alive, and took eleven pills to kill myself.

I wanted to be dead before Wolf got home. In my death I wanted to say, "NO! You don't have the power and you will not rape me one more time!"

After taking the handful of Ativan I laid down and quickly fell into a deep sleep. When he came home and found me, he must have figured out I overdosed. Somehow, he woke me up. Then, he forced me to walk for miles across a bridge to the ocean and back to his house. I was out of it and could barely stand. He never called 911. I only remember bits and pieces of that night. I remember nothing of the days immediately following.

One Step at a Time

I had overdosed to the point that, for a while afterward, no thoughts were going through my head. In a strange way, it was a welcomed silence.

Surviving this overdose somehow cured me. In my heart I felt that if I could survive eleven doses of an already toxic and dangerous drug, God must have wanted me alive.

It's funny. Only weeks earlier, I was feeling so dirty and ashamed that I swore I would never be clean again; but on this day while in the shower, I found within me little more than a mustard seed of renewed faith to cry out, "God, make me clean again."

God spoke to me immediately, clearly saying, "Get off of the medication."

I knew immediately which medicine He meant. Maybe even more wonderful than hearing that one instruction was noticing how God's voice was now much stronger than Satan's. Hearing Him so loud and clear and present, I knew He still loved me and wanted to help. I was broken and wrong about so many things, but God, my Lifelong Friend, was right there just waiting for me to ask Him for help.

I called my neurologist and told him he needed to get me off the Ativan as quickly as possible because it was driving me crazy. He didn't question me and agreed right away, but warned me it would take months to safely wean me from the drug.

Now that I had a real plan, I felt hope arise. No matter what you are going through, hope will pull you through. I had hope because I remembered that God is my Friend. If you ask Him to, He will rescue you. I am living proof of this.

I knew that getting my life back to any type of order meant I had to listen to God's voice and not Satan's. To break the cycle that led to suicide, we had to slowly change my thoughts and retrain my mind. God walked me back out of the darkness one step at a time. He didn't give me a long list of complicated things to do. He gave me just one simple step to complete before showing me the next. Gradually, as I took action in obedience to what I heard God say, things turned around.

I am no longer ashamed or afraid of speaking about what I did because it's part of my journey. Besides, I cannot change the past. God is with me and forgave me for hurting myself. He understood my brokenness. He pulled me through so I could help others.

Please be careful not to judge. We all have breaking points and people can become suicidal for many reasons. Given the right amount of pain and pressure in the right areas, you would break too.

If you feel like you *are* breaking, please cry out to God and those around you for help. Call a friend or hotline and talk to them. Let someone know what you are thinking and feeling. God wants to help all of us get rid of depression, anxiety, and suicide clouds. The Bible tells us if we seek God, we will find Him. He is always close to those who are crushed and broken in their spirit—not to leave them there, but to lift them up.

Chapter 10

Path to Freedom

Your word is a lamp to my feet and a light to
my path.   (Psalm 119:105)

During the hot Florida summer of 2003, it took me everything just to stay alive while an attorney worked hard to expedite my disability case. Because of the severity and frequency of my seizures, she was able to push past the red tape and get my case before an administrative law judge in a year and a half. At only twenty-three years old, we knew that winning a disability case was not going to be easy.

I gathered all the doctors' notes and medical records I could. I took a basic skills test to see where I stood on basic subjects. I scored at about a seventh-grade reading level, fifth-grade for math, and I was writing at some sort of high school level. This was horrifying to me because only a couple years prior, all my aptitude scores were at least high school level and I had passed a GED exam in Ohio. To make things worse, I had become abysmal at spelling even though I had always been a great speller. I even studied some Latin in high school.

I gathered my test scores and GED from a couple years prior so my attorney could demonstrate to the judge that I was not only disabled medically, but debilitating seizures had caused me to regress mentally and intellectually. Retraining my brain would be a difficult undertaking, and one I simply lacked the capacity to do while every day was a fight just to stay alive. We even had a vocational expert hired by the government testify that there was no job I could work safely. Still, even with all our evidence and efforts, there was no way to know whether we would win the case, and after two separate hearings, things weren't looking good. The judge was grumpy, irritated, and impatient. All the evidence had been presented and it seemed the odds were against us.

My lawyer and I left the courtroom following our second hearing and started down the long gray hallway. I wasn't exactly sure what had happened but was caught off guard when she turned to me and suddenly announced:

"We won! We won both parts!"

We ... won?

Unsure of what to do with myself, I asked, "So ... what does this mean?"

My lawyer replied, "You're going to get your SSI (Social Security Income) back paid from the date you originally filed, and then you are going to start getting SSDI (Social Security Disability Income) every month."

I blinked. She continued, "This will qualify you for Medicare, but it will take a while to kick in."

The outcome of the case also meant I could take a letter of the judge's decision to obtain Florida Medicaid while I awaited Medicare benefits. Not many young adults can qualify for SSDI because it requires work credits. I had worked so much as a teenager and young adult that I had the necessary credits. Only God could have prearranged such a miracle!

I was ecstatic. Something *good* was happening.

My first goal was to send money to the ones who cared for me over the years. They had all sacrificed so much for me that it was the least I could do. After that, maybe I would have enough money to pay rent and escape Wolf for good.

Changes

Soon after winning my case, I found out that I was pregnant, but after becoming extremely ill with pneumonia-like symptoms, I miscarried. I was still weaning off Ativan and suffering almost constant withdrawal symptoms—shaking, sweating, headaches, and insomnia, but through it all I stayed focused on getting free.

By December of 2003, I was almost totally off the Ativan. God had directed me to a holistic doctor who scheduled me to begin a yeast-free, sugar-free detox diet starting in January. I think weaning off sugar is as difficult as Ativan, maybe worse! I even missed out on sweet Christmas treats, which is a big deal for me and my family, but I was determined to get healthy so I could think for myself and be strong, rather than weak and preyed upon by men.

Once I was totally off the Ativan and on the path to freedom, I planned to meet with my rabbi and his wife, and Wolf. I was afraid, of course. There was no telling how he would react. Wolf valued his reputation above all. It only mattered to him what people saw, not what happened behind the scenes. I was anxious but knew I had to press on and tell them. The night before our meeting, God gave me a dream.

I saw an angel taller than my door holding a sword almost as tall as the angel. The sword was shining, its tip touching the ground, and looking ready to swing at any moment. I kept this in my mind as I went to the meeting.

I told them that Wolf was forcing me to have sex with him. I confessed that I had given in to him on occasion but it was never how I wanted to live my life. While I was wishing I had used the word "rape," because it would have been more accurate, the rabbi's wife interjected, "The word 'predator' comes to mind." God showed her.

Despite the severity of my report against him, Wolf never threw a fit. Rabbi remembered observing a medical situation when Wolf refused to heed a family repeatedly urging him to stop. I was sure he would catch the red flags next time. I didn't go into all the details about Wolf's control, being zip-tied, or the depths of his abuse. They knew the most important thing—I was being raped.

Rabbi wanted to help the both of us. He recommended an in-patient treatment for Wolf, and agreed to help keep us apart.

Now that I was off the Ativan, I was able to think more clearly. If Wolf called or showed up where I was staying on my grandparent's property, I would notify Rabbi immediately. Rabbi would then call Wolf and persuade him to leave. After at least a month of Rabbi's interventions, Wolf finally gave up and left me alone. He still stared or made weird comments if he saw me at the synagogue, but his hold on me was gone.

As my health improved, I was invited to sing and play keys with the praise team. It was delightful to be serving again. I was finding my way back to freedom.

I stayed away from Wolf, off Ativan, and persisted with my yeast detox diet. I didn't spend much time on screens. I just ate, slept, cooked, dallied around the apartment, read my Bible, and wrote songs. I went to therapy for the trauma. It was at this time that my new neurologist at Shands invited me to the electrolyte study. Before my long sabbatical where I would experience deep emotional healing, God made sure I was stable physically. It was a gradual process, but I didn't care. I was finally moving forward.

While on sabbatical, God had placed safe people around me inside a new church family. The young mom who was cutting my hair was able to give me a lift to service on Sundays. It was during this time of healing from Wolf, from Ativan, from all the years of sickness and trauma, that I had the major encounter with God described in the first chapter. As you can see, the events leading up to that encounter involved many steps and quite a bit of process. God was teaching me, loving me, and causing me to grow. If I hadn't entered into the process as best I could, I don't know that I would have had that encounter.

Six months later, I looked so different that my former rabbi didn't recognize me. The rest, the food, emotional healing, and time in God's presence had completely transformed my appearance.

I think I experienced the deepest inner healing during altar calls at church. I wondered whether it was becoming too much, but He kept telling me to go. *Can't we do this a little less publicly?* I would ask; but it didn't matter. Every time I went forward, God moved on me to heal me deeply and release me of trauma. Sometimes I just worshiped quivering and in tears as I remembered all I had been through and how God delivered me. After service I often lingered, letting God minister to me while everyone else socialized and fellowshipped.

I am amazed by the simplicity of this path to freedom. Many steps were challenging, but as I trusted God's leading, He continued to make a way and provide for me at every level.

From four years old to nearly forty years later, my Lifelong Friend has proven to be faithful. He has never failed me but continues to work on me daily. I don't know what you are going through, but God has a path to freedom for you, too. Just cry out and ask Him what He would like you to do. He never gave me a long list of tasks. He gave me one thing, and if I focused on that one thing with my whole being, I could press through everything else. I am living proof that with God and a mustard seed of faith, even the most dangerous situations can turn around.

Catch the Red Flags

Some of the worst control and bondage I have ever experienced came from people that I met at a church. Church is awesome in so many ways, but even there, you must remain alert because Satan can be anywhere disguised as an angel of light, or a wolf in sheep's clothing.

> *Be sober [well balanced and self-disciplined], be alert and cautious always. That enemy of yours, the devil, prowls around like a roaring lion [fiercely hungry], seeking someone to devour.* (1 Peter 5:8)

Don't shut your eyes to the reality. This evil is happening. Predators are everywhere. They might seem nice. They could be at your church, school, or medical facility. Assume they are out there seeking the young, weak, or vulnerable. Do not be afraid, but likewise, do not ignore the red flags. Keep your eyes and ears open. Ask God for discernment to recognize and follow His instruction when something is not right.

1. Watch out for children, pre-teens, young women, and single moms with kids.

2. Pay attention to who is working in or near any of these groups.

3. Watch for anyone who seems overly interested in "helping" a disabled person or child.

4. Ask God to show you anyone who might be dangerous.

5. Always operate in grace and humility. Do not go on a "power trip" trying to take down everyone in your community whom you deem a threat. Remember, God loves and died for us all, and God watches over us all.

6. Pray. God will give you clarity and peace and show you if something is wrong, and if you ask, He'll also give you the wisdom and instructions for how to handle it.

Many years after I came through this, God gave me a song called, "I Said, NO! (Why Did This Happen to Me)?" I am free now, but so many are stuck in abusive relationships, sex slavery, sex trafficking, and human trafficking. I remember them daily. Every time I sing this song I am reminded that action is still needed for them to be rescued. These are the lyrics:

I said, "NO." But he wouldn't listen.
I said, "NO." But he didn't care.
He said, "No means yes, and yes means no."
Oh, baby how I love you so.

Oh, God, why did this happen to me?
I miss living when life was carefree.
Why did this happen to me?
My world was shattered when he stole from me.

Cause I said, "NO!"

I cried out, "God, make me clean again."
Set me free. From this bondage and sin I'm in.

Cause, my no means no and my yes means yes.
My voice will not be silenced or suppressed.

Oh God, why did this happen to me?
I miss living when life was carefree.
Why did this happen to me?
My world was shattered when he stole from me.

Cause I said, "NO."

I said, "NO," but he wouldn't listen to me.
But now I'm strong. I am free.
God's power through my voice has crushed the enemy.
Now I'm strong. I am free.

Satan no longer has any power over me.
Oh, God, take all that's happened to me.
Come and set all the innocent free.
Wrap them up in a warm blanket of Your love, daily.

Hear their cries,
Just like You heard me.
Let them know, You are coming to set them free.
Because You hear, when they say, "NO."

Chapter 11

Pressing On

> *Brothers and sisters, I do not consider that*
> *I have made it my own yet; but one thing I*
> *do: forgetting what lies behind and reaching*
> *forward to what lies ahead. I press on toward*
> *the goal to win the [heavenly] prize of the*
> *upward call of God in Christ Jesus.*
> (Philippians 3:13–14)

*B**eep! Beep! Beep! Beep!*

Ah, the lovely sound of my five-dollar alarm clock from Wal-Mart while it's still dark outside. I'm not annoyed … not really … because I'm slowly but surely getting my education.

Each day, I walked out to the front of my grandparents' property before dawn to catch the medical bus and eventually make it to school around 8:00 a.m. The long ride would have been perfect for catching up on schoolwork, except it was always so bumpy that I could never study on the way. We all have much to overcome and endure if we are going to succeed in life!

It was now fall of 2004, and for the first time in a long time, I felt relatively free of seizures, free of Wolf, and free to pursue a healthy and productive life. I still had flashbacks every time I saw a silver pickup truck, but I was focused on my education and not easily thrown off course.

The only downside was that Wolf was attending the same college. I prayed often that I wouldn't see him. The one day it happened, I was waiting for the bus. He saw me and looked shocked. Why wouldn't he? I'm sure he never expected to see sick, helpless, vulnerable Laurel in college. Nevertheless, there I stood, probably looking better than he'd ever seen me and doing just fine without him. He didn't even try to bother me. I wasn't weak and sickly anymore. Harassing me now would have been a bad idea.

God soon blessed me with a room I could rent about one mile from my college. I was so happy! Thanks to that single mom from church and her willingness to share her space with me, I no longer had to ride for hours daily on the medical bus to get to classes. She was so loving, accepting, and exceedingly patient with me. Sometimes we would sit in her living room and talk about God for hours. I miss her and our conversations. She was a music teacher and played keyboard for our church praise team. God has always been awesome about surrounding me with the right people for each season of my life.

Before I could take college level courses, I had to take remedial reading and math classes. I loved my reading professor. She was great and also pretty tough. The amount of work she assigned was overwhelming at times, but good.

It was good to create some structure. When recovering from trauma, daily routines can be extremely beneficial. Routines and good daily habits help to keep you focused and also provide a sense of safety in the familiarity. Each day, I went to math and reading classes in the morning, and worked on homework in a computer lab through the afternoon. In the evening, I returned home, ate dinner, did more schoolwork, and went to bed—on time. I never stayed up late because I had to get up early for school.

In addition to catching up on math and reading, there was one other set of skills that I seriously needed to improve—namely, social skills. I could relate to people on the medical bus and the medical field, but what about everybody else? It had been a while since I had any social life outside of church services. I decided to throw myself in, full throttle. I applied to write for the college newspaper.

As I met some other students and connected with the accomplished writer, journalist, and professor in charge of the school newspaper, I made the mistake of telling her I was writing a book.

"What makes you think you are a good enough writer to write a book people will actually want to read!" she barked.

I was stunned by her cold and aggressive response.

She continued, "It is prideful to think anyone would actually be interested in what you have to say!"

I burst into tears.

"I *don't* think I'm a great writer at all, but I know God wants me to share the story of His friendship and all He brought me through."

She began to change her tone and made a comment about religion.

Still a little shaken but amazingly not backing down, I explained, "God wants people to know it's about the *relationship* with Him, not just religion."

You know what?

This professor and I got along great after this! She often had to rearrange my articles before they went to print, but never told me to stop writing, despite the fact all my peers were better writers.

In a relatively short time, my Lifelong Friend had turned everything around. I was pressing forward in every area and He was there to help smooth the bumps along the way.

Nothing's Easy

Nothing came easy for me.

It took me three full semesters of math just to get up to college level algebra. I had to work hard, pray, focus, and stay positive and determined to fully understand the material rather than just get by with a passing grade. I think I made As and Bs in all my college prep and college math classes, which seemed impossible because it was not my best subject. I had decent writing skills but had trouble remembering grammar and spelling rules. Everything took a lot of effort, but I was happy to be well enough to relearn the education I had lost and press on towards my goal of getting off disability.

Being both disabled and a first-generation college student qualified me for a comprehensive grant program that supported my entire college education, up to and including a counselor. Sometimes my counselor advised me to slow down and take fewer classes, which I was glad I heeded after my doctor took me off hormone therapy due to a complication and ordered me the "D&C" procedure (dilation and curettage). This was all fine and well except that during surgery I was injured. A deep cut had caused me to lose so much blood that I became anemic.

It was a nightmare.

After missing three weeks of college algebra, I had to catch up on all materials plus complete the final exam with barely two weeks left of the semester.

By the grace of God, some help from my professor, and a math tutor, I was able to catch up and score a B for college algebra. Of course, I was frustrated that it wasn't an A, but it's a miracle I was even able to finish.

My Lifelong Friend was doing so much so fast that I barely resembled the girl of just one year prior. No one could tell I had been raped or severely depressed or suicidal. Of course, I was still processing pain as things surfaced when no one was watching or at church services. When I felt God working on me, I just let Him. It was by no mean an easy process. Every day as I pressed on by God's grace to be free and whole, He met me where I was and kept chipping away at the wrong belief systems. If pain surfaced at school or somewhere public, I would just find my way to a piano and play it out, or to the bathroom in the music building and cry it out.

God was at work in music, too! I had prayed for over a decade to get voice lessons so I could sing better for God. I felt like I wasn't using my voice fully but didn't know how to change it. God opened the door for me to take voice lessons in college, and I even got a scholarship for it!

To be in voice class, you had to also be in the choir, which turned out to be both fun and serious. The training involved sing-speaking and some other techniques that made a huge difference for me as a vocalist. Even now I miss it terribly. It was there I began to find my real singing voice and also greatly improved my piano skills. I remember thinking how easy a math test would be compared to learning a new German piece of music. My brain always tries to rearrange the tempo and notes once I learn a melody. In fact, my brain tries to rearrange it while I'm just reading the music for the first time.

Because I was still dependent on others for transportation, I was often on campus from morning till night. Members of Student Government started hanging out with me in the cafeteria at lunch. After a while, they asked me to join them. I didn't want to get behind in school, so I just signed up for the beginning level of service. In Student Government, we learned a ton about communication and leadership. I loved being able to serve other students.

I can scarcely describe all the doors God opened for me during this time because they were so numerous. Every day I felt happy inside, experiencing the strength to do more than I had done in many years. God was moving fast, but there was still a process. To function and succeed I had to remain sensitive and obedient to His voice.

My mental and emotional state became the exact opposite from when I was tied up, controlled, and suicidal. Even though I had yet to really understand my purpose in life, I knew God had a solid plan and was with me in it. Much more, I knew He wanted me.

To know my Lifelong Friend was fighting for me every minute of every day was all I needed to keep pressing on, and I *would* press on in Him. I would press on in emotional healing; press on to keep forgiving; press on to get my education; press on to get my degree; press on to learn social skills again; press on with health battles; press on to get scholarships and grants; press on against naysayers; press on even though I knew the abusive boyfriend was attending nursing school at the same college; press on to keep finding rides; press on no matter how things looked.

My God had given me the ability to live, move, and find stability in every area of my life. As I stayed determined to become the woman God created me to be, my Lifelong Friend gave me the strength and courage to keep pressing on.

Sean

It was vital that I experienced personal healing and restoration before engaging relationships once again. In 2006, while visiting with a cousin in her home, a man came over for dinner and to talk about youth outreach.

"You know," my cousin began, looking at me with a most curious expression, "he's a good Christian man, Laurel. You should at least get a shower and do your hair and makeup!"

I was not looking to date anyone or trying to impress him, but I knew she would annoy me until I caved, so I did pull myself together—*a little*—before he came.

He arrived and the evening went fine. I felt he was a nice guy but wasn't instantly drawn to him. Over time, he would be around the family more and I started getting to know him.

In the fall of 2006, just a few months later, we got married.

You may think that was too fast, but courting someone while you're in a relationship with God is different because He shows you the way if you'll only pause to ask and listen for His response.

At that time, both of us were in the right place with God and in our lives, and we knew we were supposed to be together. Sean and I have been married for over fifteen years now. He is strong in every area I am weak and has always done his best to keep me safe. We also have a daughter, and together we are amazed by the countless blessings and faithfulness of our Lifelong Friend.

Life isn't easy.

Nothing in my life has come easy.

Maybe you're discouraged or depressed by all the things happening in your world. Maybe it seems impossible to do what God has called you to do. I am here to tell you that God will walk with you every time you take a step of faith. If I had listened to what was said about my brain, the low

IQ score, and the low likelihood of success, I would never have attempted college. When you don't know what to do next, just start asking, seeking, and knocking on the doors, and God will open the ones He wants you to walk through.

When you have been beaten down by Satan, circumstances, yourself, and others, it can be easy to just give up. Don't. Your heart is beating right now. You are still breathing. Therefore, you have a purpose that God wants to help you fulfill. You can finish college. You can do the work God has for you. Agree with God and take baby steps to start. God won't ask you to take a big leap until He knows you are ready for it.

More than making me able to work for Him, God wanted me to know how much He loved and wanted me. Knowing God wants you, accepts you, and loves you will strengthen you to press on through every obstacle. You will succeed if you don't give up.

One day, when I was thinking back on how my Lifelong Friend answered my heart's cry for voice lessons, I wrote this song.

Song of Love

I've always wondered what it would be like to know how to sing, andI've dreamed of bringing my voice to my King.

A song of love, a song of love, a song love to You, my King.

I've always wondered what the angels in heaven sing like, andI've dreamed of bringing heaven's music to earth.

A song of love, a song of love, a song of love, to You, my King.

I have prayed for so many years.

And I have shed so many tears.For I didn't know how to truly sing to You, my King.

A song of love, a song of love, a song of love, to You, my King.

Chapter 12

Speak Up, Stand Up!

> *Open your mouth for the mute, for the rights*
> *of all who are unfortunate and defenseless;*
> *open your mouth, judge righteously and*
> *administer justice for the afflicted and needy.*
> (Proverbs 31:8–9)

Your voice matters.

If you have been abused or raped, please speak up and tell someone safe. If you're working from a hotel, being trafficked, or have a pimp, it is better to contact the National Human Trafficking Hotline instead of contacting local police. Law enforcement officers are not always trained to recognize the difference between criminal activity of a prostitute and someone who is being abused, brainwashed, or physically forced.

In the case of domestic violence or abuse, definitely report it to the police. The prosecutor's office needs multiple complaints or hard evidence to be able to bring a case to court. They cannot go after everyone, but if you speak up and your abuser does this to someone else and then they report it, your combined reports will help the police demonstrate a pattern of behavior.

I did report Wolf to the police, but there was nothing they could do because it was just my word against his. Going to the police may not have saved me from Wolf at the time, but it may have protected someone else down the road, someone maybe even younger or more vulnerable. There are also resources through Victim Advocates and other organizations who provide support. My case is not classified as human trafficking, but I help in this area as God leads because rapes and abusive patterns like I fell into with Wolf commonly lead people not only to more abusers, but into the hands of traffickers.

No matter how much I tell you about what God has already brought me through, it would sound peachy compared to what I hear and see happening to children, teens, and adults today. Slavery is real. Slavery is still happening. When I began my recovery, there were few resources for the level of help I needed. I could never just stay in one safe place for long because no one but God Himself could handle the trauma and exhaustion of caretaking with all the seizures and complications of my life at the time. Today, more and more resources are being developed to fight this fight of modern-day slavery. Often, children are targets. Knowing only a tiny speck of what they might be going through is horrifying. It's not enough to sit on the sidelines and assume someone else will intervene. It takes a village. We all need to step up and work together on a unified front to prevent, rescue, and provide support for recovery. It takes God's divine intervention. It takes teamwork. What will you do to help end slavery and bondage in your community? This last chapter is a call to action.

Pray and ask God how He would have you get involved:

1. What will God give you the grace to do right now? Can you pray for one of the organizations working

daily in this battle? Can you pray for God to show you what is happening in your area?

2. Can you give a one-time or monthly gift to an organization?

3. Can you contact your local Human Trafficking Task Force to see if there is more you can do in your area?

Here are some ideas to get you started:

1. You can get basic training on how to spot and report potential or actual sex/human trafficking.

2. If you like to read, you can get the TIP report from the US State Department and find out more about what is happening nationally and globally. I learned in the 2019 TIP report that foster children and teens are a target for traffickers in the United States. This is important to know. It seems obvious, but knowing how criminal organizations are operating in your country and locality can help you keep an eye out.

3. Watch. Watch for kids' and teens' safety when they are out playing with friends. Predators are always on the prowl, so we must always be watching and know they may be in every neighborhood, even the ones that look safe.

4. Churches and houses of worship: This is a huge area for people to be connected to each other and God, but predators are almost always here, too. Hopefully,

they are getting the help they need. We want people to find Jesus and be restored so they don't keep hurting others. Watch carefully in all ministries. Single moms with kids or teens are a target. Young people with disabilities are also a high target along with children's ministries, youth, college, and young disabled adults. Any weakness can be exploited by a predator. Don't live in fear. Just keep your eyes and ears open and ask God for discernment.

5. If you are still a student in high school or college, you might be able to start a club at your school to help spread awareness and raise funds for organizations.

6. Don't give up! This is the key to success.

Resources:

1. Glory House of Miami: www.gloryhouseofmiami. org

2. Miami-Dade County Coordinated Victims Assistance Center 305-285-5900

3. Hope for Justice- www.hopeforjustice.org

4. End It Alabama www.enditalabama.org

5. Tim Tebow Foundation www.timtebowfoundation. org

6. For info on health and wellness: www.zachbushmd. com

7. Ancient Minerals Bath Flakes & Oil at www.enviromedica.com.

8. Joyce Meyer, Hand of Hope, Project GRL www. joycemeyer.org

If You Enjoyed This Book, Will You Help Me Spread the Word?

There are several ways you can help me get the word out about the message of this book...

- Post a 5-Star review on Amazon.

- Write about the book on your Facebook, Twitter, Instagram, LinkedIn, – any social media you regularly use!

- If you blog, consider referencing the book, or publishing an excerpt from the book with a link back to my website. You have my permission to do this if you provide proper credit and backlinks.

- Recommend the book to friends – word-of-mouth is still the most effective form of advertising.

You can reach me at: www.laurelkasco.com